*Wh*oliness

The Unified Pursuit of Health, Harmony, Happiness, and Heaven

james f. schroeder

Foreword by John Wood

WHOLINESS

The Unified Pursuit of Health, Harmony, Happiness, and Heaven

Copyright © James F. Schroeder

Printed in the United States of America [1]

ISBN: 978-1519577696

Cover Design by Sara Sexton

To my parents,

Who first taught me to see the whole person in myself and others.

Every education teaches a philosophy; if not by dogma then by suggestion, by implication, by atmosphere. Every part of that education has a connection with every other part. If it does not all combine to convey some general view of life, it is not education at all.

—GK Chesterton

Table of Contents

Foreword

For several years now I have tried to inspire other people to live a life of holiness as I struggle to seek that path myself. I haven't encountered a lot of people out there saying that holiness is their goal, but I have found that almost universally people want happiness. What I have discovered in my own life is that holiness and happiness are the same thing and so we all want holiness, whether we realize it not. God is a loving Father, and a father wants his children to be happy. Holiness is simply becoming who God created us to be. But how do we do that?

As an eye doctor, author and speaker, athlete, and a father of four small children, I often find myself off balance in my life and in my search for holiness. Sometimes I get overzealous in a certain area of my life and begin to neglect my duties elsewhere. Sometimes I get so consumed with my work that I neglect my own physical, intellectual, emotional, or spiritual needs. Whenever I start to get off balance, a strange thing happens. If I put all my effort into speaking and writing, I suddenly lose my focus and start to struggle with speaking and writing. The one thing I devote all my attention to suddenly becomes stagnant and frustrating. It has become clear to me that if I put off praying, or exercising, or eating healthy, or spending time with my wife and kids, then I feel less focused, less energized, and less happy.

I never put this all together until I met Jim Schroeder. Dr. Schroeder is one of those guys whose words and witness just instantly makes you want to be a better person. As a master psychologist, he has an uncanny ability of helping you see your own thoughts and make sense out of them. He helped me realize that running makes me a better speaker and writer. Prayer makes me a better husband and father, doctor, author, and athlete. A healthy lifestyle makes me a better doctor. And vice versa on all those things.

When I read this book, light bulbs began going off everywhere. It was so simple, yet so profound. In my search for happiness, which led me on a search for holiness, I realized the main ingredient is wholeness. I've been trying to bring Christianity to ordinary everyday people. Dr. Schroeder brings ordinary, everyday people on a journey to discover their whole self, and they end up at Christianity. The message of Jesus Christ is timeless and genius. The truth about Christianity is not just one aspect of our lives, it is the one essential ingredient to every aspect of our lives. Holiness does not just involve the soul, it involves the body, mind, will, and intellect as well. Christianity makes us better at everything we do and everything we are.

In this book, Dr. Schroeder courageously draws the connection that the things that make us holy are the things that make us whole. He is not interested in what is popular. He is interested in what is true. His work, research, and experience as a pediatric psychologist uncovers a truth that Christianity has been teaching for two millennium. I hope his words will challenge you in a new and exciting way. I hope it will encourage you to question what is common and seek what is truly healthy, no matter how difficult it may be to give certain things up, for every journey toward something is a journey away from something else. Every day I echo the words of St. Claude de la Colombiere to keep me on the right path, "Make me holy, Oh God, and do not spare me in the making. For I want to be a saint, no matter what the cost."

Open your heart, mind, and soul, and allow this book to lead you to the peace, joy, and happiness that your heart yearns for. Jim Schroeder has a writing style that is engaging, reflective, poetic, and packed with a truth that will have you saying over and over, "He's right. Deep down I know what he is saying is true. Now I have to apply these lessons to my life." Do it. Be healthy. Be happy. Be holy. Be whole.

—John R. Wood, author of *Ordinary Lives, Extraordinary Mission*

Preface

Very often we find ourselves struggling and disconnected from the person who we are called to be. We go looking for solutions in different places, only to find that sustained progress and growth does not seem to come. Meanwhile, as our lives seem more compartmentalized and arranged, we slowly begin to slip away from the holistic existence that all of us desire. We seek happiness, health, and harmony in circumstances that don't endure, and settle for superficial solutions that do little more than get us through our day.

The purpose of this book is to explore and explain how the search for health, harmony, happiness, and holiness is directly equated to our pursuit of wholeness. Throughout the centuries and in our Christian tradition, this message has been spoken about in different ways. Yet, it seems that all of us to some degree continue to compartmentalize our lives. This not only detaches our faith pursuits from the different aspects of our being, but also each of the core dimensions from themselves (e.g., our psychological existence from physical existence, physical from social, etc.). In the process, we often find ourselves languishing instead of thriving, far away from the person we are called to be.

A primary focus of this book is to synthesize patterns of thought from an academic, theological, and experiential perspective into an understanding of just how Christianity is ultimately about the pursuit of wholeness in the image and likeness of God. This book is not intended to be prescriptive, but rather a reflective, experiential look at how various types of knowledge and authentic experiences can provide a guiding mirror for our own lives. I will attempt to engage the reader in the process of this search, partially using my own experiences and that of others. The purpose is not to create solutions, but instead uncover keys that will guide us through the process of our own unique calls to *wholiness*.

The introduction and chapter one bring the reader into the encounters we are seeking and the initial questions and issues that must be addressed. Chapters 2-7 make up what I consider the foundation. These are tasks and challenges that every human being must confront, especially in today's culture; otherwise, no real progress can be made in our search for *wholiness*. Chapters 8-11 address the physical dimension. Chapters 12-14 address the social dimension. Chapters 15-17 address the psychological dimension. Each of these chapters will weave in the religious, Christian dimension. The final two chapters culminate in an examination and reflection of how all of this comes together in our pursuit of *wholiness*. The epilogue is meant as one illustration of our perpetual search for divine mechanisms present on earth.

To you the reader, I promise a few things. The first is that the chapters to follow are intended to challenge you on many fronts, and also challenge conventional thinking as it pertains to life today and our religious beliefs. Much of what is written is countercultural in all aspects of the word. Two, although I seek to acknowledge the broader societal trends with which we reside, I hope that what I have written conveys an unwillingness to accept them unless they provide for better health, harmony, happiness, and ultimately heavenly pursuits. Third, I promise to give focus to topics that are important, even if they might be regarded by many as mundane, difficult, or unapproachable. Ultimately, my hope is that through the authentic experiences and reflections posed, it will be helpful in your own journey of discernment. For all these reasons, I feel that the book would be most beneficial if read one chapter a day, so that you the reader have time to discover just how the *wh*oliness I describe pertains to your life and your calls. Thank you for entering into this discernment with me.

Introduction

Being

The glory of God is man fully functioning.   —Irenaeus

I awoke to a flickering light. Sitting up, I thought for a moment I had left my head lamp on. As I listened to the varied sounds of breathing around me, I discerned that the light was coming from the campfire that had stubbornly refused to go out. I stepped out of the tent into the breeze of a perfectly cool night. The stars brilliantly looked down upon me. Making my way to the bathroom across the gravel road, there was only silence. The day before, Steve and I had taken our four oldest kids for a wilderness adventure in the German Ridge area of the Hoosier National Forest. We had hiked up hills together, prayed over meals, and watched them as they joyfully scrambled over rocks and hopped through creek beds. Laughter was never far away. Even when complaints of tired feet crept in, they were suddenly entranced by the allure of hidden caverns and secret passageways. The next morning, a brief rain shower would usher us out of camp to a nearby country church. There just the prior Tuesday, my great-great uncle Charles, the last of a great lineage, was buried where my great grandmother laid in rest. I had never been to St. Mark's. I wondered just how many in our blood line prayed and praised next to me as I contemplated the extraordinary meaning buried in our ordinary day.

Lying in the tent, listening to a nearby owl bring the sleepy forest alive, the multiplicity of my being seemed as near as the dirt beneath my head. We had come in search of brief adventure for our kids, and ourselves. Along the way, I found myself immersed in the physical, social, psychological, and spiritual realities. The rocky, rooty trails spoke to my toes as the smell of pine spoke emanated to my soul. My mood lifted as I gazed from the ridgeline into the hollows and hills far beyond. Conversation ensued about many matters, of simple topics and challenging days, and of persimmons littering the forest floor and acorns scattered galore. And the spirituality oozed forth, from formal prayers and Mass-time traditions to layers and layers of ancient stone.

In reflecting on my perpetual search for well-being and communion with others, I can't help but sense that we will not find it unless it is in raw form. Physically, as we move further away from the rhythmic patterns of sleep, and of satiety, and seasonal discomforts to a life that is dictated by the search for convenience, and comfort, and frivolous complexities, I wonder just how our bodies will know what it feels like to meet our earth? Psychologically, when I seek to avoid, and pull back, and resign; socially, when I seek to disconnect and detach for long periods of time, I wonder how I will meet myself, and others, in true form? And spiritually, when I find worldly excuses to explain and rationalize what I do, and forego opportunities to look beyond, I wonder if a laugh will just be a laugh, if a death will just be a death?

Often when advice is given and received to improve each of these four dimensions, it is done in resignation. We're told to eat our raw vegetables, but often begrudge that it is no fun. We are given strategies to decrease our anxiety, but feel it is just too much work. We know that we should set up times to talk to each other

2

about important matters, but a text seems much less daunting. And when we are given ways to pray and sacrifice, the abstractness and mysteriousness of it all leads us to seek assurance in other ways.

And still, we all seek greater well-being, harmony and rhythm. We all seek a renewal that the forest knows so, so well. But in seeking this out, the layers between us and the dirt under our feet gets thicker, and more soundproof, and more contrived. It is understandable. So often we have been mistreated, and scorned, and felt physically ill and tired, and despondent and afraid and agnostic because what we desire the most spits in our face, abuses us, and says goodbye. Then we run from the forest vowing to never come back.

When this occurs, it seems that we depart from our humanity into the façade of an existence enclosed by many walls and locks intended to keep us safe and unembarrassed. But somewhere, the owl calls us in the night even if we do not discern the source of her reverberating voice. And she tells us that in running, and seeking impenetrable shelter, our humanness, our soulful, fleshy, imperfect humanness, is slipping away. In the darkness, the "whoooo" asks just that question of us. "Whoooo are you?"

The answer is chilling. We are hydrogen and oxygen combined, bright, red corpuscles of blood, sinewy fibers of unfathomable strength, and enough neurons to span the world many times over. We are industrious thoughts and deep feelings and desires with tremendous hopes in search of purpose and understanding. We are faces and gazes and hugs and tears of many generations who have raised their children, and loved and warred through eras and epochs and eons of years. But above all, as Pierre Teilhard de Chardin once said, "We are not human beings having a spiritual experience. We are spiritual beings having a human experience."

In removing ourselves further from our being incarnate, it seems impossible to expect that we will ever come to know just "whoooo" we are really are. The person that we will come to know will only be an approximation of the being that resides inside. We will look in the mirror, and wonder who that person is, and who that person is to become. We will find ourselves staring at a stranger whom we did not let into our home, who has been slowly stealing from us in the night.

But if we seek authentic well-being of whatever sort it may be, then we must resolve ourselves to go back home into the dark, forbidding silence that we have run from so many times before. We must confront the owl in the night, and yell back, "It is me." We must leave our phones, and heaters, and televisions, and insurance policies behind, and seek out the snow storms when they arrive and hills when they begin to flood in our everyday lives. We must do the hard work, not because we have to or because we should, but because we interminably believe a sighting will come. Only then will a shadow emerge in the twilight of the morning, eerily familiar from days harkened past and decades yet unknown.

In doing this, it is time we let go of the status quo, and not simply jog regularly because it is good for us and pray in superstition. We must eat in ways that let us traverse the mountains and speak to others so honestly and compassionately that we are startled by just what we just said. We must confront the anxieties that limit us so that one day, a walk past him no longer evokes fear, but courage within. And we must embrace our spiritual,

4

religious being so that when our own wake is just days away, that impossible, supernatural tale does not haunt us because we have turned our back on its eternal call.

It is time to embrace the four dimensions of our being. It is time to lay awake at night and say "Thank you, God" for this miraculous ability to breathe and for these people breathing next to me, who sometimes drive me crazy, but give me the opportunity to love. It is time to go home where we began—to play in the mud and seek out answers to questions never thought answerable and resolutions to conflicts seeming unresolvable. If we do, in depths of our cortex and in the chambers of our heart, we will begin to find our way back home. Home to a dimension that we have always known, and yet never truly knew, where fear of any kind has no room in the place where we will go.

1

In the Long Run

If my ship sails from sight, it doesn't mean my journey ends, it simply means the river bends.   —Enoch Powell

Our journey begins. In many ways, the journey that begins right now is the one that began this morning, and will continue tomorrow for generations to come. In actuality, it began decades and centuries ago, far before we were born. It is a journey of authenticity, a journey of emergence, a journey seeking unity and truth. But make no mistake. This is a journey of an unusual kind. Of epic and eternal proportions, it never leaves the being that it resides. The destination is the center of a soul, where noise and clatter and distractions of no kind exist, where the image that appears is perfectly synonymous with the outer being that resides.

This trek begins with a few premises of which you may or may not agree, but with which are necessary for us to seek a better understanding. The first foundation is based on a phrase that we have all heard. It is that each of us is made in the image and likeness of God. It is the understanding that everything about our being was designed with a particular, unique purpose even if many never go fully realized. This premise is not based on a proof. It is based on a necessity; otherwise this voyage stays ashore. The second premise is that although we are one being, we are composed of many parts (or expressions). Although each part serves particular functions, they are interdependent, not independent, of each other. They consist of unique qualities and dispositions and features. But the full expression of each individual part cannot occur without the others. Attempts to refine or develop certain parts without heeding the needs of the other will likely lead to disappointment, injury, and ruin for the whole being. Similarly, abandonment or neglect of certain aspects always carries significant risks for the individual. The third principle is that a person's contentment and salvation, and that of future generations, is directly associated with a person's seeking to fully realize God's image for each of us through the dimensions (parts) of our being granted by our Divine Creator. Just as our body is a temple where our soul resides, and our mind is an avenue through which our interdependency is expressed, so it is that the wholeness of our image only reaches fruition when the dimensions emerge in their purest form.

These four dimensions are the social, physical, psychological, and ultimately, spiritual aspects of our being. Some may quibble with the selection of these four basic elements. Certain people may argue that the intellectual dimension is distinct in itself, or that that the social and psychological dimensions are much the same. These are valid contentions. Yet a close examination, and reduction of humanity to its sparest components strongly suggest that these four dimensions uniquely underlie all, and form unique parts. Each dimension realizes itself before a child is even born, just as a fetus soothes best to the sound of a mother and can feel the presence of her fingers against the womb. The physical expression of our body occurs in *concrete* form, whether it is a footprint in the sand or an arm extended to the sky or a nerve firing in the heel. The social representation occurs in *conduit* form.

It is a current of energy and connection and often conflict that traverses between beings of all sort. Feelings often arise from individuals, but their social transmission occurs through eons of time and space. The psychological manifestation of our mind exists in *conscious* form although many of our thoughts, feelings, and understanding occur through *un*conscious means. But whether it is a search for intellectual understanding or emotional awareness, there is a degree of consciousness, whether or not humanly perceived, that defines this dimension.   Finally, the spiritual realization occurs in *consubstantial* form, that is, possesses the same essence of divinity. We are beings of divine origin, where divinity resides within us, and through which our humanity is ultimately called to subsume for all eternity.

Whether some question the completeness or parsimony of these dimensions is not of great importance here. What is of importance is what happens when we remove ourselves further from these cores of our being. We live today in a world of specialization. Gone for most is the Renaissance existence where individuals routinely sought out expertise or experiences in a variety of fields or disciplines. In our current era, whether it be in healthcare or education or artistic pursuits, increasingly we see a focus on specializing within minute areas. In some ways, it makes complete sense. The human mind, body, and experience can be incredibly complex, and understanding both the nature of the problem and the proper solutions often requires significant expertise in specific areas.

But what happens when this philosophy permeates our daily existence? What happens if we start to see the parts of our being in isolation, and treat both solutions for problems and methods of refinement as independent of

8

our other dimensions? Furthermore, in addressing each part, what happens if we not only abandon the wholeness of our being, but also seek out artificial and avoidant strategies to address the problems within the parts themselves? If you believe that the initial premises I proposed are self-evident, then we must conclude that a departure from a holistic existence will have dire consequences. Furthermore, it suggests that when we go looking for solutions to our problems, we will often go looking in the wrong places, and repeatedly find ourselves frustrated with our lack of progress.

Let me use four examples to further illustrate these points. A middle-aged man finds himself eighty pounds overweight, and his bad cholesterol and blood pressure continue to rise. Type II diabetes has set in, and all signs spell serious cardiac risk factors. He goes to his physician for the typical treatment regimen, and it repeatedly fails. He keeps eating in the unhealthy ways he has for over two decades. Meanwhile, he has never dealt with physical and emotional abuse that he suffered as a young child, and he remains anxious and depressed. His first marriage ended in divorce and his current marriage seems little more than two people passing in the night. He stopped doing things with all but one friend years ago. He was raised Catholic, but now considers himself agnostic because he doesn't understand how an omnipotent God would ever allow for bad things to happen to him and others. But all that he and his doctor see is a man at risk for dying a physical death. It appears that his physicality may be the least concern.

A twenty-something female presents to a psychology clinic for depression and generalized anxiety. Although of seemingly average weight, her diet has consisted of fast food, cheap snacks, artificial drinks, and candy since an early age. She has never engaged in physical activity unless forced by her teachers and has not seen a wooded trail in ten years. She sleeps about five hours a night while frequently spending the majority of her evenings online. Her parents are married, but communicated little while growing up and she reports that her current relationship with them is rather detached. She has the reputation of being rather demanding in social circles, and never joined any groups or clubs through her schooling years. She goes to a local Christian church, but prays only when things are going very bad. She presents for a psychological problem. This may be the least of her concerns.

A father of four children comes to his priest stating that he does not feel close to God, and is lost in his faith. He says he has a number of friends, but times together usually revolve around beer, poker, and sports, which leads his "old lady" to roll her eyes in disgust. Communications remain rather superficial. He finds himself increasingly fearful about going outside of his routine. Always somewhat anxious, he now regularly experiences panic attacks going into stores, but tries to act if nothing is wrong. He regards psychologists and their "psycho-babble" as useless, not willing or interested in seeking out professional help. Instead, he resorts to drinking at various points during the day to "take the edge off." Once a star baseball player in high school, he now finds himself forty pounds overweight and increasingly inactive. He presents for a spiritual problem. Faith may be the least of his issues.

Finally, an adolescent boy complains to his counselor that he has no friends. Although his weight remains within normal limits, for years he has been binging and purging food after witnessing domestic violence between his parents for much of his life. Once a young boy with natural athletic talent, he stopped playing sports years ago and became a gamer, often spending upwards of seven or more hours a day staring at a screen. His mother has tried to get him involved in a youth group at their church in addition to going to weekly services. He tells her that church is too boring and prayer never helps anyone. He says he doesn't have anything in common with them anyway. He is not even sure if God exists. This boy complains of social alienation. This may be the least of his worries.

Within each of these individuals, we find pieces and chunks of ourselves. We find our tendency to deny and compartmentalize our problems into what seems most salient and accessible at the time. Even if we were asked whether our spiritual problems may be associated with our diet, or our physical problems could be partially attributed to a lack of faith, we would likely scoff that these two things can't really be that closely connected. Just what does eating have to do with praying? And yet, when we lay aside pretenses, politics, predispositions, and presumptions, and begin the process of diving deep into the rawness of our soul, an awareness begins to emerge. It is the multiplicity of our holistic being. It is that what we eat (or do not eat) may have as much to do with how we pray; that who we reach out to may have as much to do with how much we move; how we deal with anxiety may dictate just how our relationships will go and our faith life will be. To be very honest, it seems rather impossible that it would be any other way. For if God truly created us from one cell (combined from two), then that cell, no matter how many times multiplied over, remains one cell in origin. And that one cell must have contained all I needed so that my conscious mind, my concrete body, my conduit self, and my consubstantial soul can articulate myself in whatever way His image defines. It seems almost preposterous that if we were designed in God's perfection, this would not apply to His image of us as a whole, not just what we have come to regard as our spiritual selves.

Our journey begins, and continues...

The Foundation

Therefore everyone who hears these words of Mine and acts on them, may be compared to a wise man who built his house on the rock. And the rain fell, and the floods came, and the winds blew and slammed against that house; and yet it did not fall, for it had been founded on the rock.

Matthew 7:24-25

2

The Fear of Fear

Worry never robs tomorrow of its sorrow, it only saps today of
its joy.   —Leo Buscaglia

By March 4, 1933, the United States was deep into
the worst depression it would ever know. Forty-eight of
the fifty states had closed their banks. Two million people
were homeless. A quarter of the workforce was
unemployed. Industrial production had declined by more
than 50% from the three years before. The nation had
much to fear. Up to the podium rose a man, crippled so
badly by polio that for the rest of his political life, he would
be physically supported by others as he spoke to our
country. It was the first Inauguration Day for the person
who would later become the only United States president
to see four terms. Few knew him well, and even fewer
had any idea just how he would change the fortunes of
those listening. Within minutes of his opening, he would
deliver a line that became one of the most quoted
presidential remarks ever. Franklin Delano Roosevelt
proclaimed:

> So, first of all, let me assert my firm belief that the only
> thing we have to fear is fear itself—nameless,
> unreasoning, unjustified terror which paralyzes needed
> efforts to convert retreat into advance.

Most of us only know the middle piece. But its full
unveiling speaks more deeply about what FDR was trying

to say. The line speaks to the kind of fear—that which is unreasonable and immobilizing—which leads to avoidance of what is needed to move forward. Although FDR was not a psychologist, his proclamation echoed the underpinnings of cognitive-behavioral therapy, which would eventually become one of the most well-researched psychological modalities in treating anxiety and depression. It isn't that situations like the Great Depression shouldn't evoke fear. But when fear and anxiety become the guide, and avoidance and immobilization become the response, the ensuing negativity then cycles into an intrapsychic tornado.

What is clear is that even in the worst of situations, whether the death of a loved one, natural disaster, or chronic illness, humans react very differently. Some never let go of the fear and hopelessness. Others remain resilient despite deplorable situations. Situations alone are a poor predictor of emotional well-being. But what does predict a person's emotional health is the way that an individual thinks about the circumstances that happen in their lives. At times, cognitive distortions plague us all. By definition, cognitive distortions are irrational patterns of thinking. When these distortions are transient, people generally manage. But when they are pervasive and unrelenting, it often leads people to feel depressed or anxious. Distortions come in many different forms. For example, *catastrophizing* is a distorted way of thinking in which even small inconveniences or mishaps are seen as huge disasters. *Filtering* occurs when we focus only on the negative details while bypassing all the good things that may occur. But no matter the type, all cognitive distortions are characterized by a rigid, negative outlook. Left unchallenged, and not intentionally *reframed* into more positive thoughts, they can lead to a lifetime of dire consequences.

Unfortunately, many people understandably experience encounters with others in a fearful, distorted way. Instead of seeing them as a potential for joy, hopefulness and renewal, they are often viewed with mistrust, wariness, bitterness and derision. Fear of uncomfortable encounters with family members or situations fraught with guilt about unresolved circumstances or loss lead many to retreat to the confines of their own internal tornado. And although each person's situation is unique, fear itself is not, nor are the solutions needed to stem the tide of fear. In order to sustain true progress forward, those four dimensions of our being once again emerge. We must reach out to others in a transparent, unselfish way, and forgive when necessary. We must challenge, and actively change the distorted thoughts that consume us. We must look at fitness as an avenue for greater contentment, not an inconvenience to a comfortable life. And we must learn to pray, fervently and frequently, and know when to let go.

† † † †

Fear and anxiety have two primary functions: preservation and mobilization. In regards to preservation, this can occur at many levels. The first is life preservation. Most of us get nervous when we approach the edge of a cliff or are more cautious near a busy roadway because we are programmed to recognize that a real threat of mortality or serious injury exists if we aren't careful. Preservation can occur at a health or well-being level, which is why the thought of ingesting harmful substances can make one queasy. Anxiety can be designed to sustain our relationships, as we often become particularly cautious and wary about saying certain things during particular times. These are just a few examples of how fear and anxiety can have a preservative function.

But anxiety can also help mobilize us, as long it does not become too intense or pervasive. In fact, no anxiety or readiness is often as detrimental to performance as too much anxiety. Take playing golf for example. A complete, callous disregard for the mechanics of the golf swing is likely to lead to a poor shot. An appropriate level of focus, however, often initiated by a certain level of anxiety, is most likely to produce consistent best results as the senses are heightened and the overall attention to detail increased. Too much anxiety, though, can easily lead a good golfer to duff a ball off the tee or a basketball player to "choke" in a big game. Similar results can be translated to almost any task or activity that human beings do.

Regardless of the situation, excessive fear and worry, the kind that FDR was describing, consistently lead to outcomes of immobilization and ruin, not mobilization and preservation. Someone with intense social anxiety not only has significant difficulty engaging in day-to-day activities with others, but also experiences symptoms such as decreased sleep, stomach problems, and racing thoughts. Depending on the type of anxiety, and how often the anxiety-provoking stimulus is encountered, excessive worry not only "freezes" a person in a particular situation, it often increases feelings of negativity in related situations. For example, a person who developed a phobia of dogs from a traumatic encounter as a child not only has intense anxiety about a particular dog or species of canine.

He or she often has anxiety about all dogs that lead to negative reactions from many types of canine cues, whether barking, drooling, or even seeing a dog on television. Anxiety prevents enjoyment, and love.

It is at this point that excessive worry and fear cross over into the spiritual world. In Christianity, we are taught that the first, and most important commandment of all, is that we should love God with all our heart and soul, and worship no other God besides him. It is clear that all other commandments originate from this one. It is also said that in the bible, the most repeated phrase (including variants of) is "Be not afraid." Over and over, when individuals through the Bible are faced with suffering and difficult situations, they are told to be not afraid, and to put their faith in God. Interestingly, evidence suggests that today, anxiety is the number one psychological complaint in both youth and adults, and in the United States it has risen significantly over the past hundred years[1,2].

If unwarranted and excessive fear persists, then loving God fully becomes an impossible proposition. As St. John says (1 John 4:18), "There is no fear in love, but perfect love drives out fear because fear has to do with punishment, and so one who fears is not yet perfect in love." From a young age, we were taught that God created the land, and the sea, and birds of the sky and the animals of the land, and found them well-pleasing and useful to his ultimate creation—human beings. If the world was intended to provide us with both natural beauty/enjoyment and also objects and systems that could be used to sustain our life, then it seems that a symbiotic relationship was intended even though we know that reality often falls short of this. However, Matthew 6: 26-

18

27 also points to this relationship. "Look at the birds in the sky; they do now sow and reap, they gather nothing into their barns, yet your heavenly Father feeds them. Are you not more important than they? Can any of you by worrying add a single moment to your life span?" It also makes sense that reasonable anxiety and fear was intended for a purpose as mentioned before, as God certainly would not want us to walk straight off a cliff or keep going back to a person that is causing us serious bodily harm.

But what happens is with unreasonable fear, or fear that was never addressed after a reasonably anxious response, is that it prevents us from using all of God's creation for both beauty and utility. In other words, social anxiety prevents us from truly loving our neighbor. A persistent, debilitating fear of storms can leave us bemoaning wind and rain, not recognizing the critical, life-giving effects of both. A fearful response to people of different ethnicities or cultures can invalidate the beauty each individual can behold, regardless of color or culture or creed. And so, if anxiety prevents us from truly embracing many forms and manifestations of God's creations, from the simplest to the most complex, then it is reasonable to conclude that unreasonable and excessive fear prevents love of God himself. We should certainly be in awe, and fear God's omnipotent powers, but many theologians and philosophers alike have noted that we must learn to see God's handiwork in all that exists around us. As C.S. Lewis noted in one of his personal letters,

> A great many people (not you) do now seem to think that the mere state of being worried is in itself meritorious. I don't think it is. We must, if it so happens, give our lives

for others: but even while we're doing it, I think we're meant to enjoy Our Lord and, in Him, our friends, our food, our sleep, our jokes, and the birds' song and the frosty sunrise.

If all of this holds truth, then a final presumption emerges. If we must love and worship God above all things, and above all, we must not be afraid, then all of this suggests one thing. Addressing unnecessary anxiety is not only the most important psychological task that most of us face, it appears that addressing our unnecessary worries may be the most important spiritual task we are given. Working through needless anxiety increases our ability to meet the demands given to us, allows us to embrace our individual callings, and ultimately, meet ourselves, others, and our Maker in the manner intended. When we do not willfully take the necessary steps to reduce anxiety—spiritually, physically, socially, and psychologically—we are left in a precarious state where our fear, not His call and His love, dictates step after step. Almost all of us, at different times in our lives, have asked God in prayer and pleading to rid us of a particular fear or apprehension. It can be demoralizing and disheartening when fear persists even in fervent prayer. But I wonder. Maybe God's willingness to allow this fear to remain has a more important purpose, one of critical self-improvement. At times, it is as if He is saying that in our prayers for deliverance from a particular fear, He has given us all the tools we need for that difficult task if only we look more closely within those dimensions of our being, and be willing to take on the hard work required.

3

The Root of All Vices

Everyone thinks of changing the world, but no one thinks of
changing himself.
                                        —Leo Tolstoy

It was the fall of 2004. I was in my last year of
formal training as I completed my internship. I began to
experience dizziness, fatigue, and dull chest pain. While it
would periodically remit, most days I felt the symptoms
and they seemed to only get worse. I started worrying,
and thinking that if I couldn't handle this year, how could I
manage a career and kids (which were later to come)?
Although I attributed the issues somewhat to stress, I
started believing the worst must be true. Something was
seriously wrong. But I told no one, not even my wife Amy,
who would have been fully willing to listen. I prided
myself on my independence, years away from realizing
that the life I truly desired, and needed, was a vulnerable,
interdependent one. I was too proud to admit that I was
struggling. I wondered if people around me noticed. For
me, pride had manifested itself in greater admiration of
my own capacity (in comparison to what others could
offer) with a focus on self-preservation for fear of "losing
face" or status with others.

One day I decided it was time to go see a doctor.
He ran a number of tests. They all returned negative.
Although I was relieved to some degree, part of me still
wondered if something was wrong. I was still having a
difficult time crawling outside of myself. Then, sensing my
stress, he offered a prescription for Zoloft, which seemed

appropriate at the time. I declined it (not knowing if I would later reverse the decision). He seemed surprised, but I just felt that there was more to understand before I was ready to take this step.

I began to look around. I noticed that I had gained some weight over the previous few years. My two-a-day Coke habit (facilitated by free soft drinks in the lounge) couldn't have been helpful for my GI system. I rarely drank water. My diet started to look much less healthy than I surmised it to be. Even though I prided myself on being an active person, I realized that cool weather (and putting the bike away) brought about extended sedentary periods. Slowly, I started to acknowledge my own vulnerability, and that I may not be as independently smart and capable as I had thought. I began to acknowledge this to Amy (and eventually others), who had been much more vocal about her own particular struggle at this time. Gradually, over months and years as I detailed in my book, *Into the Rising Sun*, things started to change. But I sensed this would be a lifelong process.

As a young child growing up in a Catholic family and in Catholic schools, I periodically heard about those seven deadly sins: lust, gluttony, greed, sloth, wrath, envy, pride. I was taught they were deterrents to my eternal salvation. But it wasn't until years later, through my own struggles and those of others I met through my professional work, that I began to realize just how much they constrained my own psychological well-being, and my life as a whole. Born of typical, universal urges, the scars of each of them made flesh—in individuals, in families, in communities—increasingly seemed to rise to the surface, almost omnipresent in our modern world. Signs abounded of the obesity crisis, of STD epidemics and never-ending on-screen flaunting, of intense, unabated anger and violence expressed in schools and public forums; increasing gaps resounded between poverty and wealth (with debilitating debt in the middle) all of which started to look less like personal selections, and more like transgressions committed against ourselves, ironically in pursuit of the same goals. Those being, real life, real liberty, and the real pursuit of happiness and health.

But it wasn't until years ago, mired in my own psychological struggle, that I began to sense why I heard pride described as the "root of all vices." On a superficial level, I perceived that my pride denied me the opportunity to see that I was doing anything wrong or harmful at all. In my inability to recognize my slothful, lustful behaviors, in my obliviousness to my own envious, greedy underpinnings, I only saw one path. The one I was on. So when I started to do things that were hurting me, or others close to me, I was blind to a different route. I thought that my answers lay within. I was wrong. It was only when I began to look elsewhere, and forewent the idea that I knew it all, that I could start seeing things more clearly, as others might have all along. New options surfaced. In trusting myself less, I began to trust myself more—increasingly more conscious that I was always at an intersection, not a lonely, windy road.

As I worked (and will always work) to palpably shed the layers of pride, something else started to emerge. One night in bed, I told Amy that if somehow I could only focus on not disappointing God (instead of myself and others), how freeing that would be! I knew that perfection for this goal was not possible, but slowly I worked and prayed that my statue would be chipped away. Something began to emerge. My expectations began to relax in curiosity of what divine goals might look like. I began to let go of the pride that I could do it all on my own. Still, I continued seeking out the truth and embracing big challenges. I started to see the possibilities that came if I really acknowledged where I failed, and how I had done wrong. My statue started looking different than I expected. My roads began travelling in directions less planned, and often not trodden.

Something else emerged: an unforeseen freedom. Freedom in acknowledging that I might be wrong, or ineffective, or misguided altogether. Freedom from worrying less about how I appear and more about the beauty I can profess. Freedom in seeking out a truthful existence while knowing that others may not like what I say or do (and they might be right to feel that way), but could still respect how it was done. The more this discovery of freedom occurs, the more I strive to embrace two things: transparency and unselfish intentions. In and of themselves, these hopefully harbor less and less of my sinful desires. I know I fail, but I hope that I am getting better—at least in knowing when I go wrong. But I know that my pride remains my biggest deterrent to the health and happiness that I desire. Don't get me wrong. I still work to find joy and gratitude in the efforts that I make, especially when they work out well. I just hope to let go of the pride that assumes I am responsible and deserving of it all.

Because when pride resurfaces, I feel anxious again that I am not living up to the expectations of myself and others. I worry that things will not work out. I feel depressed that what I am doing seems to matter little at all and that people don't care. I feel paranoid that others might call me out as a fraud, or just odd. I start making excuses about why my greedy, envious, gluttonous desires aren't really that bad at all. And then things just start going wrong.

It seems no way to live. I want to be free—free of mind, free of heart, free of soul. I don't want to be weighed down by thoughts of myself. I want to live in the now, ready for what is to come. I want to be acutely aware of all that lies within, between, and beyond. I want to experience the intense beauty when it comes in its purest form, refusing to resign myself to shadows and images of the real thing. I want to be free to live as life calls. But it seems I must pay a price, and die to myself so that what rises up is better than I could have known. It is time for my pride to move along.

† † † †

If anxiety is the biggest deterrent to love, then pride is the biggest deterrent to truth. But the challenge with pride is that understanding what exactly constitutes it is not an easy thing, especially when explaining the concept to children. Most of us learn from an early age to be proud of what we do and the affiliations we have, and show great "pride in our work." These statements come from multiple sources. One, we teach our kids the importance of recognizing that hard work can pay off. When they do this, we feel reasons exist to be proud about what they (and we) have done. Secondly, we also want to show that we are happy to be part of a family, community, school, or any other organization. For example, when someone wears a shirt emblazoned with a school or team logo, they are showing pride in being part of this group. We sense, and teach, that there is something of great value about being part of a group that stands for principles, progress, and tradition that we feel are important. In many ways, pride in these contexts is about encouraging excellence and camaraderie.

But then we hear that pride is "the root of all vices", and the more prideful we are, the more defended and unwilling we are to recognize all of our imperfections. This exists in the same way for organizations or entities, too, such as being too proud in being a U.S. citizen, and thereby, not being willing to acknowledge when our country has made serious mistakes. We have all heard the proverb (Proverbs 16:18) "Pride goes before destruction, And a haughty spirit before stumbling." It clearly implies that not only can pride result in arrogance and close-mindedness, but left unfettered and unaddressed, it can lead a person or organization to eventual injury, failure, and ultimate demise. That's what happened to the Romans right? They became so entrenched in their excess, and prideful that they were living the "high life" that they never saw the assassin from within.[*]

So how do we resolve this issue? First, we have to go back to the root of the word itself. Depending on what

---

[*] A similar confusion can be found with forms of the words (self)-righteous(ness) and piety (pious). Both can either be used in a positive or negative connotation. Depending on the usage, righteous and piety can either be used to denote a person who is virtuous, devout, or honorable, or an individual who is pretentious, haughty, or hypocritical. For example, when Christ was presented at the temple, Simeon was described as a righteous and devout man, as one who fully gave himself to God. But then later Luke 18:9, Jesus begins the parable of the Pharisee and the Publican. As Luke notes, "And He also told this parable to some people who trusted in themselves that they were righteous, and viewed others with contempt." Here righteous is clearly used to denote arrogance and hypocrisy.

root you use dating back before A.D. 1000, whether *pryde*, which reportedly meant both "bravery" and "pomp", or *prūd/prūt* which meant "arrogant", or *prūthr* meaning "stately" or "fine", it is clear that there has been a multi-faceted (and possibly) confusing situation for some time. But what is clear with all of the connotations of the word, as the Latin word *prōdesse* denotes, is that something is designated "to be of worth." This designation may be purely the result of arrogance, such as someone who tries out for American Idol because they believe they are the next Whitney Houston (without the tragedy), only to be told that they would do the world a favor if they stopped singing for good. Or their pride could be a source of reality, as when Susan Boyle captivated the world in 2009 on Britain's Got Talent with a voice that belied her simple appearance.

If pride designates something of worth, whether in actuality or not, it still leaves us with the question about whether pride itself is good or bad. I think all of us would agree that it is important to recognize our worth, and it seems that scripture and Church teachings support this idea, too. As Pope Francis once said,

> All life has inestimable value even the weakest and most vulnerable, the sick, the old, the unborn and the poor, are masterpieces of God's creation, made in his own image, destined to live forever, and deserving of the utmost reverence and respect.

So, if our problems with pride are not an issue of identifying worth, then maybe it is an issue of attribution. The question regarding pride seems to be, "Just what is the source of all the good that we do, whether it is derived from service or accolades or accomplishments of any kind?" Do we take credit for this, or do we give credit where credit is due—God, others' contributions, available resources, fortunate circumstances, etc...?

Liz Murray, the author of the memoir *Breaking Night* detailing her life of homelessness to a Harvard graduate, once said something I've never forgotten in a presentation of hers I attended. She bemoaned the fact that in a movie made about her life, it was depicted that she "pulled herself up by her own bootstraps." She wanted all of us in the audience to know that despite her traumatic upbringings, this clearly was not true. Many people, including that of a dear school mentor, were critical in enabling her unlikely story to come true. In recognizing the value of others' contributions, she forewent a pride that could have easily attributed all of her success to her own doing.

Here again is where psychology merges with theology, but first we must talk about the idea of praise, especially with youth. Research[1] is finding that when we praise kids for "who they are," or as it termed "person-centered praise", it can cause definite problems. For example, let's use the circumstance of telling kids over and over about how smart they are. For kids who repeatedly struggle to live up to this description, and already have issues with self-esteem, the discrepancy between their actual performance and the praise given by others can leave them feeling even worse, and more immobilized than before. Ironically, though, for those who actually do perform at the top of their class, repeated descriptions of "brilliance" and "genius" can actually lead them to avoid challenging circumstances that might make them fail, and thereby not live up to the image that others have created for them.

28

On the contrary, "effort-centered praise" seems to work well for all kids. For those who are struggling, this type of praise clearly reinforces what they can do to improve their position. For children who excel, praising their effort lets them know that in order to keep moving forward, they must continue to take regular, concerted actions to do so. For both categories of individuals, it allows them to move away from being defined by their "reputation" (or resting on their laurels), and shift into a constant, dynamic mode of operation. It also provides—and this is critical for understanding the role and nature of pride—clear, direct communication about what they have done wrong, what they have done right, and what is beyond their control. As the Serenity Prayer says, "God, grant me the serenity to accept the things I cannot change/ The courage to change the things I can/ And the wisdom to know the difference.

Although few think of pride when they think of this prayer, it clearly speaks to the issue at hand. If we know we are of value, if we understand that our efforts, not our reputation and even our accomplishments, are most important and attainable, and if we are honest and aware of what we have been given, then suddenly pride seems to make much more sense.

God granted me free will. Therefore, it seems reasonable that I should be able to find pride in the *efforts* I make, regardless if the outcome is good. In some ways, this seems critical not just for us, but especially in encouraging a "sense of pride" in what our children do, and the efforts they and we make to be a part of something good. But, and this is a huge BUT, we must be careful about being too proud of what comes of this effort, or even what allows it to occur. I might be proud of the efforts I make to compose this particular piece in what seemed like a crazy day. But I must never forget that I had nothing to do with the neurons, glial cells, bones, muscles, tendons, and all other tissue that made it possible. I have put effort into preserving and enhancing them, for sure. But I have nothing to do with their creation and the amazing capacity that allows them to grow and proliferate. Furthermore, I had nothing to do with my wonderful parents, teachers, mentors, authors, etc... that provided me with a basis of knowledge to develop my thoughts from. Again, I may have made the effort to treat them well, and be thankful, and cooperative, but I surely had little or nil to do with their placement in my life.

When I recognize all of this, I immediately feel a sense of gratitude overwhelm any pride I may retain. Now, of course, depending on how early I had to wake up, or just how much I felt I was able to manage, pride may reemerge. And some of it, the kind that still acknowledges all the other things that had to be present to allow my day to work out, is not necessarily bad. But left unchecked, it can certainly lead us down a road of spiritual, psychological, physical, and social ruin.

Once I come to this understanding, something else good happens, too. I am better able to see the great value in recognizing when my pride hides a truth that exists, just as I expressed in my opening reflection. Sometimes when I feel particularly mindful, pride almost seems palpable, in myself and others. I can almost see it, not just in outward form (e.g., as in billowing of a chest or the prideful grab of a "beer belly"), but in a tangible distancing that arises between myself and others. When pride emerges in a self-conceited way, it seems to shut down honest communication between others, within myself, and with

God. But in recognizing its presence, it seems that a tangible choice emerges. "Do I get defensive or accusatory or excuse-laden, or do I simply articulate what I have done, where I have gone wrong, and where the conflict lies?" When this does happen, and pride steps aside at least for a moment, it is accompanied by a great relief and a sense of peace. That peace comes in knowing that in my imperfect self, I am not the architect of my design, nor the author of the play with which I reside, but simply an actor attempting to best "live out" the lines I have been given, some of which I did not know until they just appeared. At this moment, I feel I can move on to the next step I need to take, and let go of the pride in preserving the person I thought I was, or expected to be.

4

In Letting Out the Spirit Within

Everybody needs beauty as well as bread, places to play in and pray in, where nature may heal and cheer and give strength to the body and soul alike. —John Muir

In the northwest corner of Lake Superior looms the largest freshwater island in the world. It is a bastion of beauty and isolation. More people visit Yosemite in a weekend than set foot on Isle Royale National Park in an entire season. It is only accessible by a long ferry ride. Grey wolves still roam wildly across its land in search of moose wandering outside of the herd. The shorelines resemble a Maine coast with its many basins, coves, harbors, and bays all with their own unique allure. Upon arriving at each one, these inlets beg the traveler to stop for a while and enjoy their idyllic splendor. They exude a quiet harmony that runs deeply and encourages a sense of reflection and tranquility. Far away from the maddening crowd, they are a respite that remains long after one has left the island for good.

In our daily lives, these inlets are often elusive. We are bombarded with frequent stressors that often make us forget they exist. We then go in search of hobbies or activities that will take us away from the constant noise. For men especially, we are in need of outlets so that we can "blow off steam" or refocus our attention on something more relaxing and controlled than our unpredictable lives. It is a necessary thing. Those who do not have regular, healthy stress relievers often resort to habits that damage their mind, body, relationships, or pocketbooks. Outlets are also the point where electricity can flow and ideas and passions may be born. The modern world has caught on to this as well. Everywhere you look there is a new club available and new activity marketed.

Here is where outlets diverge, though. Those outlets that seek to improve and renew self, to enkindle passion, and to encourage internal growth find themselves worthy of retaining. Those that seek purely to serve as a catharsis may beg otherwise. For a long time, there has been a prevailing adage that cathartic actions, such as getting a beer when tempers flare, diving into a video fighting game, or punching away at a bag in the basement, were necessary to relieve anger so it didn't explode. But when it came time to research this accepted belief, the opposite was actually found in study after study. Those who engaged in regular cathartic behaviors were more, *not less*, likely to have difficulty managing their emotions and controlling their damaging impulses. The more they sought to just release and forget about the anger, the more likely that the anger was to take over in the days that followed. Simply put, the idea of catharsis as a healthy substitution appears to be a lie.

Which brings us back to the quiet inlets in the middle of Lake Superior. Outlets, by definition, are connections to the world toward which we can direct our energy. When we plug into one, we are transported to new and different experiences. Like the cord from our television, one form of energy is transmitted to another venue. But if the outlet ends there, little happens to transform a person. Winston Churchill understood this. During his reign as the Prime Minister of England, he wrote a book called *Painting as a Pastime.* In this book, he described his feelings that rest and release alone were not enough to provide daily renewal. He felt that one must exercise his creativity regularly, and seek to constantly develop new interests and passions. Painting was his. And so in the midst of one of the most tumultuous periods of the modern world, Churchill made sure that he never went too long without touching the brush to the canvas. Painting was more than just an outlet. It became an inlet of his soul.

When it comes down to it, outlets are best when the energy we put into them is returned, even exponentially at times. When outlets serve as a conduit of inner strength, of deep growth and reflection, and complete solitude, they suddenly transform into a source that can sustain us even through trying times. At this point, they cease to be an outlet. An inlet begins to emerge. Outlets and inlets both take energy. Only inlets return the energy even after the activity is done. When the waters in the open sea are rough and unforgiving, inlets provide a protected, even hidden, sanctuary that often runs deeper than most will ever know. At their best, when we are willing to share those inlets with our closest companions, they serve to unite us in a common goal. The goal is to improve ourselves and each other, and to teach our children the importance of seeking out inlets as they grow older.

Most truly great people have inlets. Many of these are never known except by a select few. We often assume that greatness, whether of service or leadership, is uniquely granted on the basis of talent or privilege. Often we are wrong. Greatness frequently comes through the process of daily renewal by the means of inner harbors. In our daily lives, we are in as much need of inlets as anyone else. They come in an infinite variety. They can be carpentry or volunteering or embroidery or birding or music or running or dancing or meditating. They are available to the rich and poor, lonely or outgoing, old and young. Yet, without initial and *ongoing effort*, inlets fall short of truly becoming anything noteworthy at all. They just become a noisy TV that replays the same old drama and frivolity night after night.

So how do you know if something is an outlet or an inlet? The same activity can be an inlet for one and an outlet for another. Ask yourself a few simple questions. What happens to me after I pull the plug? Does it sustain me throughout the day or week, or does the electricity simply stop flowing until the next time I get my fix? Does it encourage me to reflect, and grow, and be healthy? Or does it simply function to remove me from reality, or even worse, lead me to a path of my own demise? Does it increase the gratitude I feel, or does it create detachment or even disdain, especially for others close to me? Does it help me embrace my struggles, or does it leave me motionless, or even running, from stress in my life? Answers to the former suggest an inlet, to the latter an outlet. All meaningless outlets are not bad. All of us need silliness and detachment at times. It's just that when it comes to encouraging our own growth so that we can then grow the next generation, it seems we need to daily seek out the quiet, refreshing waters of that inner cove.

† † † †

When we speak of inlets, there are many deterrents to developing habits that will sustain and energize a person for the long-term. As I mentioned, one is energy. Even though entrenched inlets actually provide energy in return, there is a certain amount of focus, organization, and endurance required to start, and ultimately sustain a new habit or interest that can have lasting positive effects. As I will talk about later in the book, many aspects of a person's life can either provide for this energy, or make it less available. One is simply fitness, both in the type of diet a person eats and their overall level of activity. Sleep is another huge factor in allowing energy to be present, and all of us at some time or another (some more often than others) do not value or understand how important sleep is. Again, I will speak more about this in later chapters.

Yet beyond energy, other threats to "inlet development" emerge. One is the idea of how much we *value* the development and time spent on interests themselves. Take this example. A married father of three is employed at an architectural firm. Most weeks, he works at least six days and 60 hours a week partly because he wants to do a good job, but also because he picks up extra opportunities that will allow him to make more money. His wife works part-time as a physical therapist. Together, they live a comfortable existence, and do not want for anything, but he frequently worries that there will not be enough money to cover their expenses, especially the looming cost of college tuition. Over time, someone who once was a regular cyclist and loved woodworking gradually adopts an inactive lifestyle, and finds himself rarely in the shop. Although he readily acknowledges that his health has declined, he also finds himself strung out more often with work, and struggles to see another pathway. And so, the value of money (and possible promotion) clearly overtakes the values that might come with a more balanced existence.

Although most of us can identify readily with his plight, and certainly appreciate his commitment to providing for his family, his hierarchy of values must challenge us to consider if we find ourselves in a similar conundrum. Do we value financial security, or even financial excess (these two terms being very relative) over our physical/psychological health, availability to others, and continued personal growth in many other areas? In this particular vignette, I think we must ask the question: Could the family live on 20% less income, and still be as happy and secure, or even more so? Also, although all of us can literally see what dollars and cents look like on a check or tax statement, do we really consider all those factors that we can't readily see, but contribute to personal, spousal, and familial health? Clearly, we live in a society today that is dictated by money first, other priorities second. As F.S. Michaels noted in her book, *Monoculture*, evidence from all fronts, including healthcare, education, entertainment, and even home life, indicate that economics speaks the loudest. Yet sadly, because people adopt a "monoculture" (i.e., the prevailing trend of the times) without even knowing it, we often don't even realize that we are living by its invisible rules. And when we do, it can repeatedly trump the importance of carving out inlets in our own lives.

If the issue of value can prevent good habitual practices, then problem of *distraction* can derail them. We reside in a world of distractions. Never in the history of the world have there been so many things at any given time that could derail our thought. Some arise from affiliation, like Facebook feeds from our closest "friends."

Some arise from emotion, like a news story about the most recent school shooting two thousand miles away. Some result from the desire of detachment, like the newest cat video to have gone viral on You Tube. Some (seemingly) arise from necessity, like multiple texts from our brother urgently trying to get ahold of us. Some stem from anxiety, like the repeated worry that your child is not doing well at some else's house. Many arise from the unexpected events, which is especially true if you have children. The sources, and reasons, for distractions are endless. I want to be clear. Many so-called distractions are simply part of the human existence, and are necessary to our life and livelihood.

But there comes a point with each of us where pulls from every front can simply derail any concerted effort that we make beyond just surviving the day, including developing a much-needed inlet. The problem is, of course, that in order to limit the distractions, we may also have to limit our interactions with others and with the world itself. One of those worldly interactions is the phenomenon of news, and just what it means to stay informed of current events. There was a time not too long ago, prior to internet and dedicated news bureaus separate from primary media outlets, when news was largely confined to the morning paper and the evening half hour shows. Occasionally, if something really earth-shattering occurred, a newscaster would break into normal programming. Otherwise, we read a few things in the morning, and caught the ongoings of our community and world at the end of the day.

Today, though, there is not only a proliferation of news outlets both online and through television, but many people receive regular news feeds through their mobile devices. Certain people I know will provide me with regular updates that they received about a local car crash or a tragic death. These are often emotionally-laden events, which may further distract an individual from the tasks of the day. In describing this, I am not intending to sound cold or indifferent to what occurs around me. I am simply noting that collectively, distractions such as these pile up, and suddenly people find themselves exclaiming that "they can't find time" to do the things they want. But if the average American watches five hours of television a day (which they do) and 95% of people or more own a mobile device, this is just the beginning of distractions that can disrupt otherwise focused activities, especially if an individual adheres to the unspoken understanding that texts must be responded to immediately.

Distractions are insidious de-railers because each one by itself often seems rather benign. Collectively, though, they can thwart an otherwise motivated person from really enacting an inlet that will rejuvenate, refresh, and revitalize a person for the upcoming day. One of the reasons that this occurs, both in regards to distractions and our life roles, is that for so many people, detaching themselves from all of this is so increasingly difficult. Years ago, I was on a golf course with a number of friends and one of their fathers. We were all enjoying a round of golf as part of a bachelor party, and yet as we progressed through the holes, this father kept getting calls on his mobile device from his ex-wife who was in the area for the wedding. Not only was he distracted, but he also could not find a way to appropriately detach from the situation, and simply (and kindly) let her know that he would talk with her after the round was over. In the process, he became increasingly frustrated, and it ended up ruining the round for him and made it more uncomfortable for those in his group. We all must learn and cultivate the healthy art of detachment. Although easier said than done, we are no help to those around us when we find our minds nervously preoccupied by somewhere else than where we are.

Beyond value and distraction, for some people there is simply a lack of awareness that inlets not only are important, but can be life-enhancing. They either did not grow up with parents or other adults that modeled these behaviors, or they simply were so preoccupied themselves that they didn't notice those balanced lives around them. Some people even perceive inlets as selfish endeavors (which, of course, they can become if they do not adhere to the three tenets that I put forth during my initial reflection). Regardless of the reasons for a lack of awareness, people in this situation often see pastimes as unproductive and trivial.

When problems of value, distraction, unawareness, or other mechanism prevents inlets from becoming entrenched in a person's life, what so often happens is that his or her psychological state is only the beginning of the suffering. Many people without regular methods of renewal gradually become more bitter and "on edge", and either repeatedly complain about daily tasks and regular annoyances, or simply attempt to "bury" their frustrations and push forward. In either case, what happens is that relationships with others become unintentionally strained. Without realizing it, they can wear down those closest to them even as their life goal may be one of service to others. Their gift of self, although often provided in a genuine attempt, increasingly can manifest itself in a tattered, repetitive way. They can easily find themselves in "ruts" of thought and being, and wary of alternate paths. Although often beloved by others for what they try to do, they may become harder to enjoy by those closest to them. Instead of manifesting a joyous presence, the burden on their shoulder never seems to fully lift.

In the process, many of these people suffer in physical ways. It has long been known that excessive stress can lead to a myriad of negative health outcomes. It seems that simply detaching from regular stressors is not enough to refresh not only the mind and the soul, but also the body. Without an inlet, unhealthy options, such as excessive eating, smoking, and substance abuse, become a ready outlet that can carry dire long-term consequences. Vices such as these are so often sought after because, despite serious risks, they result in an almost immediate reduction of tension, and often an infusion of self-gratification. Increasing research[1] suggests that behavioral addictions, such as overeating or pornography, look very much like substance addictions. Both satisfy a particular urge or tension, possess the capacity for tolerance and withdrawal effects, and directly affect the reward centers of the brain. Sadly, a recent survey conducted by the authors (Philip Zimbardo & Nikita Duncan) of *The Demise of Guys* indicated that men use pornography almost as much as a stress reliever as they do to satisfy sexual needs. Either way, the goal is to provide for immediate gratification, not to develop habits that will sustain a virtuous lifestyle.

There is a final reason that provides resistance to a longstanding inlet. It is the issue of depth (or lack thereof) with which our practices assume. But in order to better illustrate this, I will begin with a discussion of the time-honored, and often ill-fated, pursuit of New Year's resolutions.

5

Resolving to Make This Year Mean More

To improve is to change, to be perfect is to change often.
—Winston Churchill

Every year during the last few days of December, millions of people make their New Year's resolutions. Some of the most popular are to lose weight, be more organized, quit smoking, and enjoy life to the fullest. Despite our best intentions, the statistics paint a rather grim picture regarding the success of such resolutions. For example, fitness centers reportedly see a significant decline in attendance as February rolls around. In spite of good intentions, change can be a difficult thing. According to author David Eagleman, multiple factors are associated with our inability to follow through with change, some of which we give little thought or none at all.

In Eagleman's bestselling book, *Incognito,* he tells a captivating story of the role our unconscious mind plays in our everyday life. He gives a humbling, research-based account of just how little our conscious thoughts guide our daily behaviors. He details how many daily activities are largely programmed into our brain without clear awareness. We often see things that are consistent with our past experiences and worldviews, and consequently ignore that which goes against what we believe or perceive is true. We often don't notice typos or words we are reading. We miss keys right in front of us. We may remember events very differently than how they actually occurred. But all unconscious judgments are not necessarily bad. For instance, if we had to intentionally think about routine activities like driving to work or walking and talking, we would quickly become overwhelmed. On the other hand, when it comes time to make thoughtful decisions, our unconscious mind can be our worst enemy, especially when taking on new challenges.

When faced with these challenges, few of us can resist the temptation to fall back on past habits. To effectively implement change, Eagleman advocates that, among many other ideas, we must predict what our future selves will do. If not, we will likely fail. Take, for example, the resolution to lose weight. No matter what fad is in place, it almost always comes back to moving more and eating better, and less. Many of us like the idea of eating healthier, but do not intentionally plan how we will resist temptations to eat poorly. When our houses are still filled with unhealthy food choices, when we do not plan ahead for meals (which leads to the drive thru), and when candy is still stashed at work, we are not being honest with our future selves. Many people like the thought of exercise. But when we don't plan for disruptions and inconveniences that will occur, find ways to make it fun and diversified, and stop going to bed too late, we are not being honest with our future selves. Unconsciously, it is almost as if we believe our future selves will look a lot like who we are now. Therefore, we don't do the work ahead of time needed to make real, long-term change possible.

But beyond this, there are other considerations. One is that we simply start too fast and too intensely. Thomas Merton once declared, "Happiness is not a matter of intensity, but of balance, order, rhythm, and harmony."

44

When we go from no exercise to five days in the gym, burnout is almost inevitable because it defies the typical way we work to change behaviors. Ideally, the principle of *gradual exposure with response prevention* has long been the gold standard in dealing with psychological factors, such as anxiety, associated with change. Said another way, this concept means taking small steps (as in the process of shaping) towards an ultimate goal, without allowing ourselves to avoid the fear completely. We no longer put people phobic of snakes in a room full of them (thankfully) because it usually led to complete failure and embarrassment. But we do teach them to establish a hierarchy of steps that leads to attainment of an ultimate goal, and skills to calm themselves and not avoid the steps altogether along the way.

Another flaw in our resolutions is that failure is often seen as a finality, not a step in the process. The average person who successfully quits smoking, or leaves an abusive relationship, initially fails at least five to seven times. Significant change rarely happens without failure. When managed properly, though, failure can actually serve as an asset in becoming our new future selves. When the diet crashes for a week, it may signal to us that we need to start with smaller, more manageable changes to our food choices. When our running shoes lie dormant for five days, it may be time to reach out to someone else to run with us once a week. Making changes requires accountability. One way this occurs is in developing a network of health conscious friends.

But in going deeper, much of why resolutions fizzle out is that they lack clear connections to more meaningful purposes. Losing weight to look better, or for being healthier, only takes us so far. However, losing weight to be healthier so that we can more intentionally pursue a particular calling, well, now we start to tap into a bank of emotional reinforcement that can begin to see us through the short- and long-term. Likewise, when being healthy allows us to enhance our relationships with others, and do things to benefit the public good, it is then that resolutions become a pipeline to a new lifestyle. As research[1,2,3] on volunteering has shown, we suddenly start to not just feel better, but feel better *about ourselves.* The more we realize that we *matter* to others, the better we recognize the phenomenal innate capacity that may have lay dormant for years or even decades. Through this process, we develop an increased sense of gratitude for the things that may have been perceived as mundane. We start complaining less that we have to run for exercise, and become grateful that we can do it at all. We start to recognize the sunrise for the beauty that it is, and the daily rhythms and routines for the comfort they can provide. A little ways back, I twisted my ankle while running on trails. The next few days following my injury it was difficult and painful to walk. It was only then that I was reminded just how much I take for granted the joy of walking, not just on the trails, but even to the hospital next door from where I work.

In many ways, our resolutions mirror the willful approach that is needed to overcome psychological conditions, even those of a severe nature. In committing to changes that need to be made, we must do so with as much clarity and consciousness as possible, even when these entities seem elusive. We must be cautious about agents which serve to dull us to our particular circumstances and state of mind, whether it be medications or otherwise. That is because it is critical to recognize what factors may be causing us to feel more anxious or depressed, including those that are extraneous, or superfluous, by nature. Although these factors might differ between people, they are those elements which distract us from actions or thoughts that are needed to fulfill the essential roles in our lives. Viktor Frankl, someone I will talk about later, termed this conflict "noogenic neuroses"—an existential frustration that occurs when one's focus on the trivial details causes a person to feel a lack of meaning in life. Even for more serious conditions, such as schizophrenia, it is necessary for an individual to commit in a deeper way so that the inevitable suffering of recovery to follow will carry a greater purpose beyond the pain itself.

So, this year (and this month) and as every New Year approaches, as you resolve that things will change, ask yourself a few questions; furthermore, teach your kids to do the same. What barriers of my future self will show up when February rolls around? What am I doing now to prepare myself so that these barriers do not derail my goals altogether? Second, do my resolutions have deeper roots? Will it allow me to move closer to the person I am called to be, not ultimately for myself, but for others? I encourage you to share your responses with family and friends, particularly with your children. For as Thomas Merton once again proclaimed, "We do not live for ourselves..." But in order to live for others, we must resolve to make *this* year mean more *to us* than it has ever before.

† † † †

One of the biggest challenges with the process of change is that we often fix our view on a particular outcome, not necessarily personal changes that may be more difficult to see. In many ways, this is not a bad thing as all of us need certain goals, such as a marathon finish or a desired waist size. These give us a concrete marker to pursue. But what often happens when people do this is that the moment the goal is attained, we unconsciously feel that the necessary work has been done and so we fall back into patterns that look much like our former selves. It is one reason why people who lose a significant amount of weight often gain it back. The temporary change in lifestyle was overly focused on attaining a particular standard, not revamping a lifestyle in order to allow for sustained change to occur.

The elusiveness of sustained alterations again relates directly to the four dimensions of our being. Repeatedly people rely on certain daily experiences to "sustain" them through a given week, even if these in themselves are contrary to a lifestyle desired. For example, most of us know that drinking 1-2 soft drinks or more a day can be a 5-10 pound a year habit, not to mention other negative health outcomes. But for many people, the thought of giving up their Coke first thing in the morning (or their chocolate mocha latte) is a scary proposition. Why? Because it is a guaranteed way to feel good, even if for a brief time.

Look at your own day for a second. Ask yourself just how many little activities either give you a brief rush or release tension. It could be eating a donut, smoking, viewing particular websites, combing through Facebook feeds, or any other myriad of potential options. Now, imagine removing these experiences for an extended period of time. If we are honest, most of us feel uneasy about this because we find ourselves wondering just where our pleasure and tension-release will come. And so even if there are many reasons to remove unhealthy habits, including the possibility of dying early, many people would rather know that their demise is not far at hand rather than take on the unknown of just how the rest of their days will be. Years ago, Harvard professor W. Kip Viscusi asked a group of smokers about how many years they would likely lose to a lifetime of smoking from the age of 21. They guessed an average of nine years. They over predicted, as the answer is somewhere between six to seven years[4]. Similarly, I have heard people brag countless times that they are carnivores by nature when it comes to the high consumption of red meat, even when I am rather certain that these people know the risks that they are assuming.

The fundamental challenge of change is its unpredictability. If we all knew that our efforts to improve ourselves would turn out well, and that we would still be happy without our former habits, I suspect that most would be willing to undertake steps needed (although just how hard this process is would certainly affect this).   But the problem is that we just can't know for sure whether our efforts will be in vain, and whether we will find more happiness on the other side. Some changes are rather predictable. For example, if we increase our activity level and reduce our calorie consumption, there is a very good likelihood that we will lose weight. Yet, we find ourselves questioning whether our body can "hold up" under increased activity and whether we can convince our palate to enjoy salads instead of casseroles.

I had a conversation with someone about a year ago who talked about taking up running. However, she noted that within a few weeks, her knees were hurting, and she began to worry that running was doing more damage than good. So she stopped completely (as many other people might have done). In stopping, though, she did not consider and trial other alternatives that would have kept this goal a reality, such as running on trails or utilizing a run/walk regiment. She could have researched whether certain foods can improve joint recovery (which they can) or whether blending running with spinning may have offset the pounding that she felt.

A similar thing happens in our relationships. We may find ourselves really wanting to work through something with our spouse, but initial conversations are exhausting and seem to show little progress. This might be the case for months, or even years. As with losing weight, there is no guarantee that the effort put forth will really lead to a better place. And so we quit talking about the issue, and just find alternate ways to co-exist even though both people sense that a new layer thickens between them. Frankly, we settle for less than what we both desire and are called to be. When the outcome seems very uncertain, the path of least resistance almost always is the one we return to—the one we have taken before. Sadly, though, we lose the opportunity to realize what Robert Frost once said, "I took the road less travelled by...and that has made all the difference."

When we find ourselves in this type of inertia, it is imperative that we consider a few critical things. One is simply the gift of time and energy, first to ourselves so that ultimately others will benefit. Any change that I mentioned requires significant effort, and the effort put forth simply does not come from nowhere. I will talk in the next few chapters about the three pillars of health, and why these pillars are so important for any improvement to occur. Beyond this, though, we must also look at what fills our day, and be willing to take a risk in reducing or removing habits that needlessly take up time. When Amy and I first got married, we had certain television shows that we watched regularly, and they were definitely a source of pleasure that seemed to round out a busy week. But as our years together increased, we found that we desired other things more. Our values were changing, and so slowly, television time ceded to nightly reading, writing, and conversation. Today, we probably watch less than 2-3 hours of television during an average week, most of it being Chicago Bear's football games or golf tournaments. Most weekdays, the television never comes on.

At first, I am sure there was some loss that we felt in this change, and every once in a while we find ourselves reliving the days of watching *24* when we see old promos. But to be honest, the shift away from this pattern, and any pleasure it may have brought us, is now filled with a level of contentment and meaning that does far more than "take the edge off" a challenging day. Night time has truly become a time of renewal and deeper commitment to our way of living, which is one reason that we have remained very focused on making sure that our kids get to bed at times that allow for a proper amount sleep for their age.

Although we had no guarantee that this shift would bring us to a better place, we were assured by the fact that what we were doing drew us closer to the core of those four dimensions. Our conversations became more intimate, even if at times exhausting and even frustrating.

I found myself immersed in so many different areas of study that provided for greater reflection and contemplation. Ultimately, through ways that I will address throughout this book, new pathways of writing emerged that previously did not seem to be a reality. In the quietness of those evenings, far away from the noise and controversy that the television provided, a deeper sense of *us* has emerged. Although silence can be an uncomfortable entity for many, if we are really ready to take on new avenues in our life, we must start here.

With silence first comes an understanding that change is possible. It is really hard to envision a new course if we do not first lie eyes on it in at least a moment of silent aspiration. Sometimes it is watching or listening to someone else that you know who has done the same. Sometimes it is exceeding your own expectations, and wondering if more is possible. Sometimes in prayer, in an intense moment of clarity comes the awareness that there might be another way.

As our society focuses on outcomes and accolades, we can be assured that faith focuses on effort and process. Throughout the bible, we hear Christ and other religious leaders speak about our need to become less greedy, lustful, wrathful, lazy, gluttonous, envious, and prideful. Rarely if ever do you hear them say, "You should work to only commit one greedy act a week or keep your gluttonous behaviors to 5% of your days or only look at one nude image in lust every month." I recognize that certain behaviors can be subjective (although others are not). But what all our religious forefathers do is to say, *"Look, we know that you will never be perfect as Christ was. But we want and expect that you will put great effort in this pursuit, and pray that in the process, your efforts will not be in vain as it comes to your eternal salvation. But also know that when it comes to your heavenly pursuits, this will not be for you to decide. The best thing you can do is to not strive towards a finish line that you can run through, but pursue self-improvement that will not end until you hopefully meet your fellow souls in heaven."*

Although we seek to attain perfection as He did, one of the most reassuring spiritual realities is that we are all sinners, all people laden with imperfections. Although years ago I found myself frustrated by this idea because it seemed to imply a never-ending failing, today I find myself comforted by the knowledge that my efforts to improve and change are sometimes going to fall short. But as the greatest ultra-runner of all-time, Yiannis Kouros, once said:

> Each horrid event should equip you with the necessary provisions so that you can confront the next one; it shouldn't make you yield. The continuous confirmation is that despair and hopelessness supply you with means—inconceivable at first—and they make you discover hidden unexpected powers. Later, an unhoped -for tranquility and sobriety should follow so that you may pursue your goals with precision.

Goals and targets are often a necessary starting point for needed change. But somewhere along the way, if we truly find ourselves in a better place—spiritually, socially, psychologically, and/or physically—we will find great joy in self-improvement. I was reminded of this recently by a mother of a child I know, who had gone through a difficult divorce in the past year. Despite the challenges, both she and the father had put forth great effort to make sure that this child would not suffer because of their choices. One of the ways in which this effort was manifested was through their attempts at communication. She described to me in session how she worked to avoid the easier method of texting when it became clear that there was any level of emotion involved in the discussion. At this point, she would pick up the phone and invest time in the conversation. As she was leaving my office, she noted how it felt really good to put effort into this endeavor. Although certainly never acknowledged in a finishing time, or through an article or even a concrete record, I had little doubt that this continued effort could make the difference between a divorce that ended in secondary tragedy to a divorce that might find new, positive pathways through an otherwise dreary outlook.

When people start to feel a deeper sense of contentment about the person they are becoming, regardless of specific outcomes, it is remarkable to see just how much change can occur. We have all seen it in people, when it seems that they depart from their former selves, become aware of their future selves, and yet embrace their present selves like never before. When it occurs, not in a vain way, but in a way that echoes of transcendence and meaning, we find ourselves enamored by what continues to occur. But make no mistake, that no matter what accolades or distinction this person may attain, no matter how many lives they may have served or saved, the outer, palpable outcomes of their lives are but a reflection of an inner set of practices made possible through Him, sustained in the most unassuming, mundane ways, over and over and over again.

6

Dear Family and Friends: My Apologies...

Men have become tools of their tools.
—Henry David Thoreau

Dear Loved Ones:

As most of you know, I don't carry a mobile device. The cell phone that my wife uses, and I periodically share, has no texting or internet. We aren't on Facebook. We don't tweet, but we do email and use the internet daily. Most days I bike, run, or bus to work as we only have one car. We don't have cable. We still have an answering machine that moved a close friend of mine to leave a message indicating that "The 80's called, and they want their answering machine back." Many of you undoubtedly think I (we by association) are stuck in the past, or are losing it all together. You have a valid argument.

But before I completely cede to your contentions, I hereby submit my treatise of why I (we) choose to remain in the dark ages of communication and technology. Most you who know me well will cite my frugality, difficulty accepting change, and apathy (in learning new technology) as my primary reasons for not keeping up with the rest of the world. You are partially correct. But there are some other reasons, and that is what I hope to explain here. In no random order, here is a list of excuses about why you still have to call me on a landline:

I desperately need my clarity of mind, and ability to regulate frustration and sustain attention. As a father of six kids, a husband of one extraordinary woman, and a pediatric psychologist as my official career, there is nothing more important to my life, and that of my family, than my ability to think as clearly as possible and sustain attention when needed. Especially when I see diapers disintegrating on the floor while trying to answer a math question. Like everyone, it isn't about reaching 100% capacity, but more about just trying to run on the most mental cylinders I can. With all the distractions present on a daily basis, the buzzes, rings, and dings that signify incoming calls and information would just add too much extra noise. It would scatter me like our family dinners, and even if I could appear as if I am focused on the task at-hand, I just don't think I have the brainpower to really be. Research[1] indicates humans are really poor multi-taskers; add me to that list. In a day that already has eons of demands, I worry that my efficiency would tank, and my ability to meet my most important requests would really suffer.

Silence is one of my most valuable commodities. One of the best things about riding a bike to and from work is that my vehicle is silent. The roadways may be active, but the only voice or tune is the one ringing up in my head. The quiet trip into work is a great way to collect my thoughts for the upcoming day; my ride home is a great way to de-stress, as I prepare for the noisiest moment of all—when the front door opens. Some time ago, I gave a presentation to a local group of youth ministers. Their director recalled the day he received his cell phone and pager at work for the first time, and then mourned the reality that people could (and did) contact him on his way home from work when he used to quietly process his day. Although many people use their transit time (against safety guidelines) to catch up on calls, I really do need it to catch up on my life, which seems to be running in front of me.

Mobile devices and Facebook would make me a worse communicator, and thereby a worse friend. Okay, now I hear some of you clicking on the Weather Channel. But let me clarify first. Yes, you would have more ways of getting messages to me. But I am convinced (and believe that I am not the only one) that my ability to respond, and respond meaningfully to them would seriously suffer. I know there are times I fail to adequately respond to a phone message or email, or at all. But give me many other ways that I can be reached, and my response rate (and quality) would really drop off. Part of me knows I would enjoy being more aware of all that is going on, but I just don't have the time or neurons to manage everything. And when I do talk to you, I actually want to have some real time, and capacity, to focus on our conversation and not be distracted by other things (except for one of my kids falling off a chair, of course). No doubt it would be fun to get a random text once in a while about the latest Bear's trade. But when one random text leads to twenty, and emails on my mobile device are too long or forgotten to be returned, I think my response rate would start looking like that of the grocery surveys that I receive in the mail.

I am wary of the "psychological distance X amount of information received" ratio, and what it would do to my day. I am sure others have noticed an emerging principle in the world of communication and technology. The further removed a communication gets from a direct,

57

face-to-face interaction, the more contacts you are likely to receive. Every day, people rarely show up at our front door, with the exception of an invited guest, salesman, or other random stop-in. We get a few phone calls a day. We get a decent amount of emails a day. Teenage girls average roughly 4,000 texts sent and received every month[2]. I don't think some adults are far behind. Weekly social networking feeds are often loaded with tens of thousands of new pieces of info. Said another way, the less directly people have to communicate, the more likely they will send through information.

A few months back, I was talking to a cousin, who is a coach. In his early days of coaching, he recalled a conversation with a mentor about how to handle parents who were angry about various matters. His mentor's advice was simple. If you get an email from an angry parent, always respond by clearly validating their concerns, and then asking them if they would like to schedule a face-to-face meeting to discuss their frustrations. Most will opt not to do so, unless the concern is really serious. A similar idea seems to apply with all of us. If it is really important, critical, or interesting, we will take a more direct route to let our friends and family know, although since my sister now announces she is pregnant on Facebook (love you Laura), I probably am the last to find out many things already. But the easier it gets to send a message through, the worse I get at managing it all.

The insidious role of distractions worries me. In some ways, I really love distractions, especially when things are really intense. I could easily watch Seinfeld reruns each and every night. I don't always mute the ding on my email at work depending on the day, as I don't mind my attention being pulled from the stress or mundanity of a moment, even if the ding signifies more work or nothing important at all. But as I feel pulled by many different worldly demands and curiosities, there is a stronger pull that keeps gnawing at me that cautions against letting these distractions take over.

Recently, I came across a CS Lewis quote that eloquently describes what I have been feeling. It reads (and by the way, for those who don't know the book The Screwtape Letters, the "Enemy" is God):

> The Christians describe the Enemy as one 'without whom Nothing is strong'. And Nothing is very strong: strong enough to steal away a man's best years not in sweet sins but in a dreary flickering of the mind over it knows not what and knows not why, in the gratification of curiosities so feeble that the man is only half aware of them, in drumming of fingers and kicking of heels, in whistling tunes that he does not like, or in the long, dim labyrinth of reveries that have not even lust or ambition to give them a relish, but which, once chance association has started them, the creature is too weak and fuddled to shake off.

I worry that if I am not careful, "the gratification of my curiosities" will pull me away from a greater call.

I really want to preserve my off-line life, where I find my greatest joy. Almost every week, or even more, it seems that something which was once completed or communicated off-line or by direct human interaction, is now going to an online, electronic source. Health care is morphing itself into a digital production. Schools are doing more and more through the internet. Automation is taking over in so many ways, whether in banking, shopping, or dating. And although it carries potential benefits, the reality is that each day, we are investing a little more time (and mental energy) in learning the ways of technology, and less the ways of people. I can't help but feel that people are being asked to conform to technology instead of technology conforming to the ways of people, or at least the ways we desire to truly live.

Recently, a trainer came by to teach me the initial steps of learning to use Dragon Naturally Speaking, which translates what I say onto the computer. I know some people who use it and really like it. But in being able to use this program, my trainer stressed that I would have to spend a decent block of time teaching it how to understand the way I speak, and go through steps to correct it when I was misinterpreted. If I didn't, my "dragon" could actually get dumber over time, and then it would be rendered of little use. As he was telling me this, I admit that I was feeling distracted by one looming question: "What would I have to give up to have the time?" If I knew that this would be the last technological training request for a while, I probably would have felt more agreeable. But, I am not naïve that this would be the case, as the technological world has taught me that another training is right around the corner. Safe to say it would have come from one of two main places: either from time spent with my family and others (you) dear to me, or time spent in quiet contemplation, reading, writing, or sleeping. Something about this didn't seem right.

So my dear friends and family, my "dragon" lies asleep. I am not sure if I will actually ever teach him new skills. But I really look forward to hearing from you soon, and spending joyous time together. In the meantime, feel free to stop by or give me a call on the landline. You can

Schroeder

even leave a message on our antique answering machine if you want.

Sincerely,

Jim Schroeder

† † † †

We have reached an interesting time in the history of our world when it comes to technological innovation. Never in the history of civilization have things happened so rapidly in the area of communication, whether through mass media or individual interactions. Most of you who just read my "letter" have moved far past my current state of use. And yet, all of us are increasingly faced with a few questions, starting with the most important one: *Are these changes for the better?*

In order to even broach this question, we initially have to consider two primary areas. First, we have to define what we mean by "better". Currently, when it comes to "better" as expressed by those who either market the products or those of us who use them in various ways, it generally refers to a few main ideas. One is that technology as it is developing provides greater ease and convenience. Another is that it provides greater access to a wide array of information. A third would be that it provides for more emotional, instantaneous experiences. There are certainly probably other suggested advantages to consider, but in general, it seems these three ideas encompass primary reasons why technological innovations of today have been adopted so widely. And when it comes to these three ideas, I think it would be very difficult to argue against the idea that media and technology provides astounding advances from even what we had just a decade ago.

But there are other ways to define "better", and it is possible that the advantages put forth in the previous paragraph are giving way to risks of a more a serious, pernicious nature. It is when we begin to consider this possibility that the question begins to get harder. Although this topic deserves a book in itself, here are some cursory considerations. Let's first take a psychological standpoint. Over the past 40-60 years, there are serious signs that our population as a whole, especially our young people, are developing more serious psychological issues than in prior generations[3]. Some experts have argued that we are simply more open about our emotional difficulties than before. To some extent, this seems true. But further analysis of the data indicates that this is not accounting for the huge rise in psychological difficulties. Unfortunately, it appears that as a population as a whole, we are more anxious, depressed, deviant, inattentive, and manic (to just name a few) than in prior generations. There are many factors that likely account for this increase, but media and technology innovations have been suggested as one possible culprit for many reasons.

Let's consider that "better" means in regard to social abilities. There is no doubt that youth and adults of today have never been more connected than they are now. But just like the data on psychological issues, social skills seem to be declining[4]. When I speak of social skills, I am speaking of both verbal and nonverbal communication abilities that include anything from making good eye contact to maintaining a topical conversation to using gestures and intonation in getting a point across. Ask yourself. Just how good do you feel in general that the teens and young adults of today interact on the phone and in person? Researchers are again increasingly finding links between technology use and social skills.

What if "better" is meant in regards to our physical health? As mentioned earlier, we all know that we are in the throngs of an obesity crisis in the United States, from infants to elderly adults. We also know that one of the biggest risks of the conveniences provided by technology today is that we move less to get things done, and are attracted to sedentary activities like never before, whether watching television, gaming, surfing, or otherwise. Not surprisingly, we know that the link between technology use and health concerns is strong.

And what if "better" had to do with our spiritual pursuits, most importantly our eternal salvation? Well, here probably more than in the other three dimensions, it becomes a prickly subject. Who am I or anyone else to suggest that how we use technology could actually affect our spiritual and religious lives? In some areas, such as those who become addicted to online pornography, I think many would be willing to at least consider that technology has provided an easier alleyway to increased transgressions.

But, for a second, let's not even consider the content of what we watch or listen (even as meanwhile the governing body of movie ratings have now acknowledged that significantly more violent and sexual content exists in today's films that have the same rating as they did a couple of decades below)[5]. Forget content. Let's consider process, going back to the CS Lewis quote in the opening letter:

The Christians describe the Enemy as one 'without whom Nothing is strong'. And Nothing is very strong: strong enough to steal away a man's best years not in sweet sins but in a dreary flickering of the mind over it knows not what and knows not why, in the gratification of curiosities so feeble that the man is only half aware of them, in drumming of fingers and kicking of heels, in whistling tunes that he does not like, or in the long, dim labyrinth of reveries that have not even lust or ambition to give them a relish, but which, once chance association has started them, the creature is too weak and fuddled to shake off.

The notion he puts forth is a bold one. It is not so much that the devil is in the details (where we assume he resides), but also in the distractions. Although I think that many of us understand what Lewis is saying, the question is just how much of us believe what he saying? If we are willing to consider this idea, though, it suggests that distractions might become as engrossing and debilitating as those sins for which most of us would agree are a serious concern.

Reading further into Lewis's contention, what he seems to be saying when distractions "steal away our best years" and we become "too weak and fuddled to shake off", is that we slowly lose that Godly image that we and He so desires. Even though our public professions might still be of a virtuous nature, distractions and trivialities threaten to whittle away at our ability to embrace our four dimensions without us even realizing that it is occurring. Even if we realize it to some extent, we seem to become desensitized to the changes that are occurring, like the fact that many now only check email and phone messages sparingly even though it results in more scattered communication.

Which brings us back to the question of media, technology, and "better." No one could reasonably argue that the media and technological climate of today doesn't provide greater distractions. Yet the more serious question is just what are those distractions doing to our state of being. If we are measuring progress in convenience, accessibility, and emotional experience, then we are likely to surmise that the innovations of today are taking us to better places. However, if we are assessing progress in terms of the health, well-being, and the eternal destination of each individual being, then we cannot ignore that media and technological advances are linked to worse outcomes.

It is important to note that the technology in and of itself is not the problem. Technology is completely neutral, and the components can be used in an infinite number of ways just as the components of a bomb and a bridge can be, too. The issue is how we as human beings use the technology. Some rightly argue that they use it intelligently and strategically, and so for them, technology becomes both an asset as I first noted, and risks I cited seem to be minimized. But unfortunately, and this especially applies for the generations that are growing up in a "technologically immersive" environment, it does not seem that most people are using it in this way. As one example, one of our administrators at work recently acknowledged that now that she can be reached in so many different fashions (e.g., face-to-face, email, phone, texting, Twitter, Facebook), she is finding herself increasingly scattered, tied to her mobile device, and less efficient. She certainly isn't alone.

One of the reasons that this is the case is that the technological innovations reach us at such a primal, instinctive, emotional level that we struggle to pull away from their lure. In referring to lure, I mean this in a multi-faceted way. On one level is the neurological tie-in. Research has indicated that a simple ding from a text or a brief screen shot taps into our brain reward and emotional centers just as substances and interactions of all kind do. We feel good, or feel affected, by the virtual or mechanical world just like we do the real world. Another connection has to do with social expectations. Even as adults, we are afraid of being left behind, and so even if we don't like the trends, we feel pulled to keep up with them. A third linkage is an economic and convenience one. Even as our mobile plans are running us into hundreds of dollars, we understand that time is money and money is time. And a fourth (and by no means last) is that the lure of leisure is never far away. The technology of today provides leisure opportunities like never before.

I speak of the issue of technology in a "we" sort of way. But as with much of what I am discussing, these decisions are very personal ones. Very personal. I can't help but think that although most people rarely consider that a new upgrade on a mobile plan, or expanded satellite service, or unlimited texting capacity is anything of consequence, it seems that there is a potential that it might bear the most serious of consequences, especially if left unfettered. Just where do we desire things to go from here? Experts suggest that our online and offline worlds will increasingly merge, and technological innovations will only continue to proliferate in our daily lives even if our being, that of our psychological, social, physical, and spiritual selves, might be suffering in the process. Is this better? Is this best?

As you consider this question, I have left one serious consideration out when it comes to changes in our current technological age. Although some might regard it as the absence of all, theologians and philosophers and even psychologists alike have increasingly seen it as a beginning to all, an indispensable quantity to the self.

It is silence.

7

The Day the Silence Died

When society is made up of men who know no interior solitude it can no longer be held together by love: and consequently it is held together by a violent and abusive authority. But when men are violently deprived of the solitude and freedom which are their due, then society in which they live becomes putrid, it festers with servility, resentment and hate.

—Thomas Merton

It is 12:30 AM. Shots of a semi-automatic rifle ring through the air. Flashes of light cascade an otherwise dark room. Vibrations course through the controller as gunfire continues amid the sounds of a landing helicopter. John's pregnant girlfriend and two year-old daughter have been asleep for some time. It had been another long day at his job. John's boss is a jerk, and most of the people he works with are annoying. Some days, just this time spent alone at night that gets him through it all, even though he knows he probably should be sleeping. But the game takes him to another place, full of beautiful, textured graphics and adventurous missions that contradict his rather mundane life. Online with his fellow gamers, he laughs as expletives ring out when an explosion lands nearby. Just slightly younger than the average gamer (34)[1], at times he feels like he is leading a dual life. What began as a fun outlet as a teen has become part of a growing trend of young men such as John who find themselves pulled deeper into the virtual world. Recently, he ventured into Second Life, and has begun to correspond with another "female" whom he is curious to get to know.

John unknowingly found himself in the throngs of "adultescence" in his 20's. He grew up in a middle class family in the suburbs, but after graduating college with a degree in anthropology, he was uncertain of what to do next. For a few years, he moved back in with his parents, and began working part-time at a nearby music exchange outlet. He pursued a few other jobs, but they seemed unappealing. Eventually, he landed an entry position at a local bank. He broke up with his girlfriend of a few years, and other relationships came and went. He found himself slipping more into online pornography, which like many of his male friends became a way to relieve stress and "take the edge off." He found himself more withdrawn, more emotionally detached, jumping from one adrenaline surge to the next, until he eventually began dating someone that he met online. Unexpectedly, she became pregnant quickly and they decided to move in together, only for the second baby soon to be on its way. Sitting there this night, staring at the screen, he finds himself wondering how he has gotten here, and just where it will lead. Along the way, he has become part of a growing contingent of young, middle class males struggling to take on the demands of adult life.

If our life is poured out in useless words, we will never hear anything, never become anything, and in the end, because we have said everything before we had anything to say, we shall be left speechless at the moment of our greatest decision.
—Thomas Merton

He is rocking forward rhythmically, seemingly oblivious to all that is around as the bus comes to a stop.

Seated next to me, I can hear the music emanating from his ear buds, sounds of outrage comingled with admissions of lust. His eyes open briefly, but just as quickly his head turns downward as he retreats back to his song. Suddenly, his trance is broken by the sound of his cell ringing in his pocket. He says a few brief words, then looks up to see his stop approaching. I watch him exit, and as he walks down the sidewalk, his head remains downward as the bus rolls by. Little do I know, but he is headed home, where the television never goes off. From an early age, it was a way of drowning out the noise of poverty, of the screams, of the gunfire, and of his grandmother yelling at him as he headed out the door.

As he grew older, music became his release. He craved rhythm where life seemed to have none. He rarely was without his i-Pod, and the musicians became his guide. Silence scared him, as if something was about to "go down." So he avoided it, and he and his friends joined the fury he felt about all the ways they had been wronged. During class, his teachers generally turned a blind eye as long as the music remained just discernible to him. His mobility only improved after he got his first i-Phone, and his friends texted and surfed throughout the day to pass the time. Unknowingly, he became part of the trend of minority youth who spend almost thirteen hours a day "linked in" to some form of media or technology, almost four and half hours more than their white counterparts.

Words stand between silence and silence: between the silence of things and the silence of our own being. Between the silence of the world and the silence of God. When we have really met and known the world in silence, words do not separate us from the world nor from other men, nor from God, nor from

Schroeder

ourselves because we no longer trust entirely in language to
contain reality   — Thomas Merton

    We walked through the valley of the shadow of life.

The previous day had been one of ups and downs—not of
a personal nature—but of a mountainous one. After
taking off on the trail the prior evening, we had started out
early in the morning as the shadows slowly ebbed to the
east over the Chisos Mountains on our way to the highest
point, Emory Peak. As the night settled in, childish
conversations reminiscent of decades past, of wrestling
javelinas and taming mountain lions, interspersed with
tales of professional pursuits and worldly concerns.

    But this morning, as we slowly made our way into
Juniper Valley, the sun was unveiling its rugged
masterpiece onto the lowly, vast expanse that lay before
us. Prickly pear cactuses and welcoming aloe plants
covered the land as our simple minds contemplated the
enormous beauty, and desolation, below. As we snaked
our way down the mountain, a small tent appeared on the
canyon floor where two travelers had hunkered down for
the night. We would not see another human being that
day.

    It had been almost ten years since my two brothers
and I had our last great wilderness adventure. Although
we had seen much of the of the beautiful landscape that
this country had to offer, in duo or with other company,
our trio had not come together for much time until we
found our way into the confines of Big Bend National Park.
As the desert sun intensified, and the harsh, unforgiving
land showed its true, often brilliant colors, the climbs and
the miles became more difficult. Like many of my past

adventures, it was during these moments that I sometimes wondered why we had not taken an easier road, one in which the toil and sweat was replaced with comfort and leisure. As the blisters began to form, and the heat of the day colluded with our entomological foes to even make a day-ending siesta a chore, the weakness in me felt tempted by a more forgiving course.

But I knew by now that I had come, and we had come, for a much different purpose. On the surface, it had been one of adventure and one of beauty, and for that it had not disappointed. But in a greater sense, we came for solitude and silence, in ourselves and with each other. We had come in search of the same tranquility that we desired and needed every day—whether in brief moments of interlude or amid the morning rise or the setting sol. We had come to the faraway land of Big Bend to remind ourselves of the joy that this solitude beheld so that when life resumed (as it soon would), we would seek to preserve and nurture it in our everyday lives. It was that same silence of understanding that we would pursue between ourselves. For although at times our conversations spoke of trail curiosities, and at times of our personal lives, much of the time our discussions were born out of the quietness of our footsteps on the rocky, parched soil and the birds swooshing by. We had travelled across the country to immerse ourselves in the comfort that came with saying nothing at all.

As we awoke to the slight morning chill, a renewed vigor found its way into my soul. Trekking our way back to the abandoned ranch in completion of our thirty-four mile loop, I once again found myself grateful for the things that only harsh deserts and long brotherly backpacking trips seemed particularly acute at reminding. Like the joy of cold water and rested toes. Later that day, as we waded through the Rio Grande with the Santa Elena canyon walls soaring 1,500 feet above, it seemed so clear. I just wanted to be one with Him, one with her, one with them, and one with myself in wherever the path would lead next—in the silence of my soul.

† † † †

When Christ was led by the Spirit into the desert for forty days and forty nights, it is worth noting that this occurred in a place of desolation and isolation. While fasting and prayer alone could have been done anywhere (although certain complications may have occurred), there is a sense that the aloneness was necessary to provide for something more. Away from his friends, family, and early followers, he faced a mountain of silence. Although we yearn to know just what happened during those forty days and forty nights, what we do know is that when it came time to be tempted, he was not only tempted by the promise of food, but also the promise of power, prestige, and affiliation. If we are to embrace his humanness, then we must recognize that this came at a time when he was little more than an itinerant preacher just beginning his ministry. He was vulnerable, and so much was left to unfold. We might wonder if the Spirit, who *led* him into the desert, knew that it was not just fasting that he needed, but silence before the temptations would come.

As we venture into the mystery of silence, we begin with a consideration of just what silence means. A first glance would suggest that it be simply an absence of noise, a quietness in the surrounding environment where we stand. It seems rather obvious that for most of us, the silence of today and the silence of previous times is much different. Artificial noise finds itself drowning out the natural noises, whether the sweet symphony of the songbird or the cacophony of the crows clamoring over a tiny morsel. The washer slowly comes to a stop. The clock ticks. The dishwasher goes into the rinse cycle. Cars pass by the front the window. The furnace resumes as the thermostat clicks in unison with the programmed command. Somewhere the owls are whooooing and the coyotes are howling. The field mice are rustling and the trees are swaying.

But whatever the sounds of our world may be, we must go deeper into the quiet mystery to understand just what silence means. We are mindful that silence is not just an agreement of our world, but a state of our mind. As we turn inward, the search for peace and tranquility begins with a moment of quiet contemplation. For some, this is a fearful moment. For others, this moment has been long desired. For certain people, it is a continuous state broken only by the experiences of the day.

Still, the experience of internal silence for all is a twinkling of awareness. When the internal conversation (or monologue) stops, we are faced with questions. Just what are we doing? Just what does this mean? Who am I? Where am I headed? Often indiscernible, the silent queries persist even if we run from their reality and become distracted by something else. However fleeting, though, silence rejects all pretenses about ourselves that we or others have constructed, and does not seem to care about the honors we have attained or the offices for which we arrived. Its questions come anew. The answers remain true.

Then, as Merton notes, we reach an intersection. Even midst the deafening falls of the Niagara or the roars of 90,000 in stadium mode, we are called to the silence of our soul. "When we have really met and known the world in silence, words do not separate us from the world nor from other men, nor from God, nor from ourselves because we no longer trust entirely in language to contain reality." It is there that silence no longer is a state of nature, or a state of mind, but a state of our soul. It seems here that we begin to wonder whether the voices we are hearing, or the calls we are sensing, are coming from another Source. Silence no longer becomes just a state of being; it becomes the beginning of a conversation that we do not know if we are having, but cannot simply just deny. In our discernment to understand what, and if God is saying, we find ourselves listening intently. Yet, we often do not know what we are listening for, and we are unsure whether what we are hearing is a product of ourselves or His Spirit rising from within.

The practicality of the matter, though, is that we are told that almost never will God force His way in. If this is so, then it behooves us to wonder just when we will provide ourselves with opportunities to quiet our mind and the world around. It is no surprise that today's world threatens this pursuit like never before, especially for those who were born to an age when noisy, vibrating devices became attached to their hip and took over their homes. Of all the serious questions posed by our current technological age, the most serious of all is this:

*Just how will we know if He is **here** if it is too loud for us to **hear**?*

As we become consumed with the noise of progress, the noise of distraction, and the noise of our frenetic lives, this question looms not rhetorically, but as loudly as it can be. Sometimes it would be nice if He would just scream at us, and maybe as C.S. Lewis once said, our pain is His megaphone in a deaf world. But do we really desire the pain that it would require for God to start amplifying His voice for all to hear? We may not always have a choice, as suffering will come in many ways. Still, it seems that much of the suffering that comes may be because our ear buds were in, and we couldn't hear him telling us that this was another wrong turn.

The Physical Dimension

Do you not know that your body is a temple of the Holy Spirit, who is in you, whom you have received from God? You are not your own; you were bought at a price. Therefore, honor God with your body.

1 Corinthians 6:19-20

8

The Three Pillars of Health

It is health that is real wealth and not pieces of gold and silver.
—Mahatma Gandhi

One of the words we repeatedly hear in personal conversation and media coverage is that of "health." In a country with serious health concerns, it is not surprising that we have become obsessed with what is healthy and what is not. Yet overall, the omnipresence of this discussion in many circles has not lead to wide scale improvement. Although some people have responded to an increased focus in this area, the health statistics remain grim.

Today, legislators, physicians, parents, and all of us struggle to understand the best ways to promote a healthy lifestyle in the midst of many temptations otherwise. Unfortunately, many good intentions have led health to become one more commodity, not a lifelong pursuit. Most of us intuitively could guess that those in the medical field declare that the three pillars of health are sleep, diet, and exercise. Many people have an idea of what they think are healthy parameters in each of these areas, although much knowledge is not necessarily based on sound science, but more so cultural and societal trends. For example, given that the plates and portions of today have grown substantially larger than they were just a few decades ago, it is really difficult for all of us to make accurate comparisons when the only reference point we have are the dishes in our cabinets or what comes to us in a restaurant or in a box.

Very often you will hear people declare that "so and so eats healthy" or "he is a healthy person", but if being overweight truly is the "new normal"[1], then these statements may only weakly correlate with actual reality. Like many judgments, there is a truth that lies somewhere in what is said, but our ability to ascertain the truth from noise can be very difficult. Certain parameters provided by our medical field can provide us with better anchors for deciding if we are truly health or not. For example, the Body Mass Index (BMI), although not without its flaws, can provide us with a rough estimate of where we rank in regards to our body makeup. Similarly, cholesterol and blood pressure readings can give us insight into whether our cardiovascular fitness is on the right track. But even these markers do not sufficiently give us an answer as they themselves have evolved over the past century. And for measures of psychological health, the question becomes even more subjective.

So, again, we are back to this question. What again is healthy? Are we even taking the right approach to looking at our own health? As I mentioned in previous chapters, it is imperative that we first look at health as a mechanism to more important things, not simply as an end in itself. We must guard against vanity that comes with a shrinking waist line not because we can't find pride in the effort it took to *pursue* this goal, but because we must be aware that the body that did the shrinking (after initial and sustained expansion) is not of our own design.

But beyond what health can allow us to do, there is something about the effortful pursuit of it all that speaks to a mysterious, yet promising endeavor that can bring rewards unknown to those who never undertake this journey. When Christ went into the desert and fasted for 40 days, it could be easily said that this could have been one of the most remarkable athletic feats ever to have been performed. Although certainly not to be undertaken lightly, the discipline and determination required for this feat is well beyond most of our imaginations.

In fact, it is these and other feats that led George Sheehan, cardiologist, father of 12, and 21- time Boston Marathon runner to declare that Jesus himself was an athlete among many other things. Jesus fasted regularly, walked long distances, ate very simply, and of course lived a very austere life. Although many would suggest that this simply was part and parcel of his times and social class, I think that we may be too quick to dismiss this reality just as we cling tightly to other realities about him as if they are critical to our faith. More to come on this connection in the upcoming chapters. But in reflecting on Sheehan's statement further, it is interesting that although I have seen Jesus depicted in countless ways, in paintings and statues, one thing always remains constant: his physicality. Have you ever seen Jesus with a gut of any kind at all?

What is clear at least from what scripture provides is that Jesus did not finish any official races, or post any sub 3 hour marathon times. But we must wonder. Was there something more with his physical practices that tied directly into more than just his faith. Take fasting for example. For centuries, many religious traditions have used fasting as a spiritual discipline. But more recently, evidence is emerging that reasonable fasting is not only good for our physical health, but can help provide for increased endurance. Many runners regularly use fasting to teach their bodies as a way of burning fat stores longer and more efficiently[2].

Through all of this discussion, we come back to this idea of health as a pursuit, but not a commodity to be attained or compartmentalized. Just as we know that we can never attain perfection (on earth) in a spiritual way, but are called to pursue it, so it seems that we are asked to consider this of our physical health, especially if it means that this journey can become a direct pipeline to a more faithful existence. This does not mean of course that we should all be training for six hours a day, as clearly for most of us this would be unreasonable and neglectful of the roles we are called to undertake. But what it does mean is that health can, and likely should, become a holy endeavor. If God provided us with bodies in His image, and we are a temple of His Spirit, then it seems just as reasonable that we should pursue His physical image of us as we should pursue His spiritual image. As the Catechism of the Catholic Church states:

> The human body shares in the dignity of the "image of God": it is a human body precisely because it is animated by a spiritual soul, and it is the whole human person that is intended to become, in the body of Christ, a temple of the Spirit (USCCB 2014, para 363).

A particular position emerges. If we believe that prayer holds promise beyond what we can readily perceive, if we believe that another human being can grace us in marriage with her presence for more than a half of century in ways that will alter the course of our life, then what kind of promise might the quest for health truly hold. No one will ever become perfectly healthy any more than will anyone become perfectly virtuous. But if you look to those who have pushed the so-called boundaries of health, you will find stories that sound more spiritual and transcendent than they do physical. Again, if we start to realize it is all of the same essence, then the false dichotomy of health and virtue dissipates as the pursuit of holiness and wholeness become one in the same.

9

In Search of a Hundred Miles of Gratitude

In daily life we must see that it is not happiness that makes us grateful, but gratefulness that makes us happy.

—David Steindl-Rast

Coldness Undone

I woke up to the sound of steady rain. Outside, four inches of snow still lay on the ground from the previous weekend. The temperatures had remained just above freezing, and the rain that was scheduled to come would likely only be intensifying as the morning wore on. But I had committed to the long run, knowing that my training was as much about being prepared for anything as it was for preparing my body for the actual number of miles to come. I wasn't sure if David would be there given his on-call schedule and the nasty conditions, and as I approached the hilly golf course at around 4:30 AM, the dissenting voices rung in my head. But suddenly, I saw the headlights staring back at me. He had come after all.

The seed for all of this had been born in the spring before. I had managed to cross the finish line at the 50 mile run at Land Between the Lakes, as thankful for its completion as I was for my second toe (on my right foot) remaining intact after repeated harsh introductions to the roots that covered the trails. Although I vowed early on that fifty was enough for me, a faint, crescendoing voice seemed to suggest that this finish line was just a step in a larger process. I was surprised, or maybe fooled, at what I had left at the end, and so I began to think seriously about going in search of a hundred miles.

But this morning, all I was looking for was warmth, as the cold, dark, treacherous hills spoke in a different way. As the rain continued, David and I rambled and slid over the descents and the climbs, and through the hollows. I was certainly thankful that my friend was there when few others I knew would understandably ever consider joining. Midst the perceived dreary conditions, there was much banter, much hilarity, and much appreciation for what we were doing. As he said goodbye ascending the seventeenth fairway, much of my run still lie ahead. The thirty-four degree rains only seemed to grow stronger. But as I crested the hill and saw three deer running in the valley below, I heard myself sheepishly say, "I know, I know, I am not alone." The snow began to create deep ice puddles, and I found one after another. The course became slicker. I was soaked, and yet strangely enough I could only detect an unfailing warmth inside. I was acutely aware of all that was going on with my body, even in the tips of my toes, and yet I found myself merging into the hills as the snow reflected the skylight from above. My joy only intensified, and I found myself wondering why I had been so blessed to experience it all—oneness with each other, with this place, with what was unknown. Gratitude permeated me, and even as I made the decision to end my run after two hours and nearly thirteen miles in order to get a little more warmth and dryness for my feet, I only knew that I had been blessed to have known it at all— in submitting myself to things that I did not understand, but increasingly sensed were true.

As the days went by, and I reflected on this run, I found myself thinking of the times that I had felt anxious and depressed. In a broader sense, I found myself musing about many I knew who had experienced serious psychological difficulties, whether manifested in the utmost control over food intake or the obsession turned compulsive behavior to cleanse oneself of contamination. What seemed to underlie much of these psychological challenges was a waning of the gratitude that was felt. It seems easy to surmise the surrounding conditions and circumstances may have much to do with this, and yet as we have repeatedly seen, situations alone are poor predictors of mental health. So often it appears that those who struggle to manage challenging circumstances, and those who remain resilient in lieu of horrible outcomes, often speak in very different tones. When we are resilient, thankfulness seems to coincide, even for the miraculous gift of life itself when the life being lived seems anything but miraculous at all. When these words are real, they are not trite, self-affirming notions — they are words spoken from the willful pursuit of something that goes much deeper than the words themselves. They are human attempts at progress in a seemingly inhumane world. But when we become immobilized, or even regress, as a result of anxiety, depression, or various mental illnesses, gratitude seems so often submerged under words of unfairness and of catastrophizing and of loss, not *gain*.

It is at this last critical point that true gratitude becomes incompatible with psychological distress. In giving thanks, we recognize a gain, no matter how small, and for at least a moment, let go of our sense of loss. But two more key departures between gratitude and psychological distress emerge. First, any act of gratitude involves turning towards others and ourselves in recognition of a positive moment in our life. Distress does the opposite – it turns against us, and often others, in a self-absorbed way. Finally, gratefulness signifies clearly that there is hope simply because we acknowledge that positive things do exist – in ourselves, in others, and in the world. Anguish and misery do not make room for hope, until gratitude appears.

Inherent ingratitude is undoubtedly born and perpetuated by many precipitating factors. But no matter how seemingly reasonable and understandable it may be, it seeks to be one of the most stifling obstacles in the pathway of recovery. If ingratitude remains a serious obstacle, maybe small steps of gratitude, in thought or word or deed, are then a necessary prerequisite to long-term recovery. And just maybe, albeit somewhat idealistically, conditions of psychological distress and uncertainty, through the process of suffering and by opening new pathways of gratitude, precipitate alternatives for hope otherwise unseen in more inviting conditions. It is a submission to a time-honored tradition in the foregoing of self at least momentarily in uncertain, vulnerable ways—moving forward into the daunting night in appreciation that light exists at all.

That morning in the cold, undulating darkness, I went in search of things I am still trying to understand, and likely will never fully uncover. In my life, there is no shortage of things to be thankful for without ever seeking out the frigid, dark hills, and yet something calls me to suffer in these small ways as each long run becomes a search for new veins of appreciation previously unseen. I really don't know. But I do know that when the alarm clock goes off early in the morning, it is time to push aside excuses, forego fleeting discomforts, and be thankful for the mind and the body that carries me into the dimly lit hills and valleys that lie ahead.

† † † †

One of the great rewards, and also one of the great disciplines, of physical activity is that of gratitude. Most of us, at many different points during a physical endeavor, have felt tempted to bemoan what we are doing, and wish ourselves onto a couch of our future liking. This is especially true when someone just finds themselves starting to take on a more physical pathway after an extended period of being sedentary. Let's be honest. Being physically active is not easy, and sometimes feels downright miserable. There have been many times over the years when I wondered why I paid a fee to enter a triathlon or a run, only to find myself sucking air and wishing for the finish line even early in the race. As my friend Mount says after every time he emerges from the swim in a triathlon, "It would be a lot more fun to be a golfing right now."

But as physical activity becomes more ingrained in our lives, and as we seek to alter our diet and other practices to aid endurance and make recovery easier, something shifts. There is a recognition that the simple act of running is nothing short of amazing. The synchronicity of the lungs, heart, nervous system, muscles, and overall skeletal structure to even make a one mile run possible is astounding enough. What allows a hundred miles to be dreamt on foot is nothing short of divine. And yet, repeatedly individuals, human individuals, have accomplished this and much greater feats, even thru serious injuries. When Scott Jurek won the illustrious 100 mile Western States in one of his record seven consecutive times, he did so after tearing ligaments on mile 44 due to stepping through a shallow rock. Physically, there is simply no way he should have even finished the race, let alone overtake people ahead of him on the way to victory. Something else clearly took over, and even Jurek's description in his book *Eat & Run* does not do justice for what must have occurred.

But with any really meaningful thing in life, there must be some struggle, some pain. When it comes to physical activity, there is a discipline that must occur to adopt it as a lifestyle, and reap the multi-dimensional benefits that it promises. The first is simply an acceptance of the commitments that have been made, and a foregoing of challenges that may ensue. Although we always have to be cognizant about pushing things too far, oftentimes we find ourselves making excuses to not exercise because the conditions are poor or the timing just doesn't seem right. For me, I work against this by reminding myself of the covenant I have made with God when it comes to my physical discipline. For example, many mornings I have woken up to a cold, rainy bike or run into work. I find myself tempted to take the dry, warm way out even though I know that God has given me all that I need to make it to my destination. At this point, I am learning to focus on each action I must take to be prepared, to be safe, and to execute what I promised to myself and God.

Once I have maintained my covenant, I work to mentally execute what I have learned from reading, reflection, and from others I know well. Seeking strength through Him, I work to harness a particular mindfulness that keeps me as close the present moment as possible and as far away from the finish line as I can be. In explaining this further, I still look forward to the promise of being in a warm, dry place, but I mentally focus on the warmth and energy I feel inside at particular moments during the activity, and the completion of simple goals, such as climbing one hill or reaching a new intersection. Over time, I have come to learn that through the effort needed to execute small goals, the larger ones will take care of themselves. Even when the outcomes are not necessarily what are desired, there is so much to be gained from the moments of intimacy and isolation that it takes to get there. It is repeatedly at these junctures, in the most unlikely of places, that gratitude emerges for the spiritual, social, psychological, and physical realities with which I am blessed.

Covenant Upheld

I stepped outside. It was a perfectly, chilly morning. The previous evening, we had attended the Chrism Mass at the Cathedral, where all the ceremonial oils of the Catholic Church were consecrated for the coming year. Easter was almost upon us. As my first few steps turned into a jog, much was on my mind. My attempt at a hundred mile run was a week and a half away. My thoughts instantly sprang to the previous October, when I set out on the first of these Wednesday ten mile runs. The half marathon had just passed, and I was in a period of discernment. For the first time in my athletic life, I had professed that if this race was going to happen, I would leave it entirely up to God. At any point, if mandated by injury or family situations or another reason, I had vowed that I would be willing to bow out—I would appreciate what I was given, but I would know that it was time to take a different course. So each Wednesday that I stepped out onto that empty road, I wasn't sure if I was coming back. And just two weeks into this particular run, I had felt my calf painfully give a mile from my work after protecting a previous foot injury. I contemplated walking, but something said to run at any pace that would get me there. So I did. By the next Wednesday, I was back, and so grateful to be.

Then the winter came, the harshest we had experienced in decades. Temperatures repeatedly plummeted into the single digits. Ice and snow arrived, only to refreeze and not leave. Many Wednesday mornings started with a simple thought: "I really don't have to do this." But deep down, as long as God kept his promise, I knew I had to keep mine. And so the dark, cold, unforgiving winter became a breeding ground for my soul. I went on until the temperatures started to break, and spring finally found its way. I learned how to run to my Lord in all that the world could bring.

This morning, over six months and 27 straight midweek morning runs later, I knew it would be one of celebration and one of thanks. Less than a quarter of a mile from home, I suddenly heard a commotion. A deer scrambled across the road in front of me. Always my companions on my long weekend runs, they had reminded me of a divine presence when no one else was around. I made my way down the hill across Pigeon Creek, a main tributary of the mighty Ohio River, onto the levee and to the Greenway trail for the next two miles. The full moon hung brightly in the western sky. And in the distance, I could see them. For five months, I had run this trail in the dark, early morning hours and had never seen anyone else. Except for them. As I passed by the older man and his three legged dog for the last time, I stopped briefly and said hello, and then asked what had happened to his trinitarian friend. The leg had been lost in an accident, and then he had adopted him. An act of love, for sure; with that, I was on my way.

I headed downtown towards that mighty river. The wind freshened in my face, providing just enough resistance to remind me of all the times that it had aided my course. As I hopped onto the riverfront walkway, the swollen body of water eased by. The full moon dropped in the sky, and I turned east toward the blazing sun. A new day, a new chapter had begun. I kept thinking about all the previous times I had found this particular path, wondering if I would come back. I wondered if I was the same man that had started this the past October. I wondered what God had in store.

As I pulled away from the river, and gazed down its timeless course for the last time, I found myself in many different places. In a moment, I was in the delivery room in December, when Louis Francis, our sixth child, was born. I was on the icy streets in early January. The wind was battering me in late March. In moments, time was eternal, and I, in each of these moments, found myself in many places, in many times that had come to be. The person I was before, the person I would become, was the person that I was now, if even for these moments. And although as always, I desired for the run to be done, my presence in His presence, left me with no other option but to savor the moment upon.

Bayard Park passed by and as I crossed Highway 41, I continued to touch the signs and rails and benches along the way. I guess I wanted to feel the sights I had seen as I let them go for some time. I approached the last two miles. I felt a slight twinge in my calf. I smiled. I had a come a long way enough to know that I would be fine, but the memory of that very early run resurfaced. As I turned left back towards St. Mary's, and the last few hundred yards came into view, I closed my eyes in prayerful motion, and briefly pushed my fear away, only to redo it again and again.

I reached the end as my thanks flooded into the street. I pointed skyward and walked towards my familiar stretching tree. The Holy Rosary bells tolled seven times in the background as so often before. I had kept the Sabbath. I had kept the covenant. As always, He had kept his. I knew that darkness would once again settle in during the following week, but for now peace reigned. I walked up the stairs and reached into my pocket for my keys. I smiled again. For on every run, I had put a dollar with my keys so that when work ended, I would have money to catch the bus home. In my mind, though, there had always been a secondary reason for keeping this money in tow. I figured that if my run went awry, I could at least struggle to a bus stop and arrive at work in this manner. But on this morning, unlike all the rest, I had forgotten the bill. And I heard a voice say, "You never needed it in the first place because I had been with you all along the way."

† † † †

One of the great scams of the 21st century is the sham of sloth. Long since forgotten as a deadly sin, it is now couched in promises of convenience, luxury, and easy. People almost brag about it as if it was a virtue, one to be promoted and developed as a means to a comfortable existence. For many, the idea of walking to the store or mowing the yard by foot seems preposterous. Why would we do this when technology offers us a much easier option? For men in particular, it seems that the value (not vice) of sloth has taken particular hold. Without sounding too curmudgeonly or harsh, otherwise able bodied men are routinely seen using riding lawn mowers on lawns that are little more than a small plot. Man caves of extended inactivity and beer guts have become a bragging point for many a man.

Rest and a periodic adult beverage are not the problem. The problem is a goal, widely perpetuated by our current media, of embracing a lifestyle that endorses "settling in" as we get older. There is no doubt that for most, physical activity in our teens and 20's is easier than in later years even though our bodies actually become more suited to endurance activities as we get older. An analysis of New York City Marathon times indicated that the times of the average 19-year-old improved until the age of 27, where they peaked and then started to decline. The striking part is that the average times did not return to average 19-year-old running speed until the spry age of...64[1]. Yes, the age when many people have already retired, except apparently from still running at a pretty good clip. But what surely happens is that new responsibilities emerge, of child rearing and professional duties, and with that has come a sense for many that sloth is not only to be desired, but actually seen as the "right of a working adult." It is understandable as having kids and a full-time job can be very tiring.

What also happens is that if the subject of sloth comes up, it quickly is relegated as a metaphor to laziness in other areas besides physical activity. And this is true. There are definitely times we seek to avoid responsibilities in all dimensions and seek out an easier route. Sometimes the energy and commitment required to have a discussion with another person may be much more than is required for a 10 mile run. Sometimes the effort of authentic prayer and self-giving is much more than required than splitting a huge log.

But before we jump to other explanations, it seems we must not forget the creature that bears our sluggish namesake. Sloths are the slowest moving mammal in the world, so sedentary that alga grows on their fur. Their metabolism is sluggish enough that it can take them up to a month to digest a single leaf. Just like sloths, there are times that we all find ourselves simply desiring a sedentary life. It will always be easier to sit on the couch than to move, especially in a vigorous way. At the same time, our life can be so frenetic that we often forget that the movements we are doing might all be actions of obligation, responsibility, and pleasure, not necessarily self-renewal and self-improvement. Unfortunately, the optional technology and convenience of today has found its way into the fabric of our everyday lives, either as a distractor or a facilitator, of an otherwise slothful existence. Without even recognizing it, we are increasingly "put to sleep" by sloth's false promises, just as its namesake often is when hanging from their trees. When this happens, it gets harder to experience just how good it feels to move and be active, and makes moving and being active just that much harder of an experience.

Sun Rise, Sun Set

The sun had risen. The sun had set. I was still running.

Earlier that morning, in the predawn hours of late April, I had set out with less than two hundred people in search of a hundred mile journey. With hand held lights and head lamps in tow, the illuminated pathway of humanity wove its way through the trails of open pastures and leafless, wooded trails. Early morning revelry and contemplative silence trotted side by side as each individual held his or her own unique purpose for taking on this epic adventure. There was a shift worker from Detroit who had arrived just hours before the race after taking off just before midnight when his work was done. There were those who had come back for retribution after last year's race became a brutal exercise in amphibious navigation. There were siblings who had come to run together. And yet, as those first few miles unfolded, the differences seem to dissipate as each of us plotted our course on the loop trail that we would see much more.

The trip since the previous July had been an exercise of discipline, suffering, and transcendence. I had arrived at Chain O' Lakes State Park just northeast of Fort Wayne wondering what this day would mean. The training had nurtured my soul, but as I came into the finish line of lap number one, and headed out towards mile 17, I was sure of one thing. I would have plenty of time to discern it all. Early in the race, I had come upon a running acquaintance who had moved out of the Evansville area, but who had kept contact with a mutual friend. He was doing the 50 miler as a training run in preparation for the Western States 100 at the end of June. It quickly became a good partnership on the trails, but as the miles continued to grow, and my body continued to feel the effects of the ever rolling terrain spent on toe, I envied his course.

As we passed through the final steps of our 2nd lap at around six hours and nearly 34 miles, I began to think of Amy, my brother, Mike, and my six kids who would shortly be making the trip to meet me. I looked forward to seeing them. It was a beautiful sunny day, and with the foliage on the trees still yet unsprouted, the rays came to us rather unabated. The run continued on. I began to think to myself. What did a hundred miles by foot mean to me? Why had I come? On my back, I carried the words, "Cure for Paula," on the same jersey that I had worn almost three years before, when "Cure for Clare" had been my running motto as my cousin struggled for her life in a battle with leukemia. She had survived, and then even learned how to thrive again. I, and many others, were praying the same for Paula, whose two little girls had seen her battle multiple stages of breast cancer on her way to stage IV. So I was running for her, and more. I was running for my family – and yet, there was more. I was running for the roles in my life, so that in my silence, in my toil, in my suffering, I would learn to embrace what was necessary to become. But, there was more, and at times the mystery of why I had sought out these endurance challenges would remain. Maybe forever. I had come to accept it. So here I was.

But as lap three progressed, I could not escape that question. What did a hundred miles mean to me? Was I willing to accept the price I would have to pay to seek its arbitrary way? A conversation with Amy of a day past kept coming back. In her last few words before I left, she had said that although I should go out like I always had in these races, in search of my goals, I should not be afraid of feeling content with what I had done. If that meant it felt complete, then I should not be afraid to be thru. And as I approached a reunion with my family, these words were on my mind. I felt content. Of course, it was no stretch that my body, like most around me, was happy to be done. But it seemed that my soul was, too. And so as my eyes and hands laid upon my family for the first time mile at 47, I whispered to Amy that mile 50 might be my last. I really just wanted to be done, and be with them.

I arrived at mile 50. And then they did what they should have done—they kicked me back out on the course. And as I turned into lap four with Amy, I felt the emotion well up in me for the first, and only time, that day. I told her I was content, but back out we went. I needed another lap to discern what the suffering meant to me. As I caught up with Mike near mile 60 and took a brief break at the aid station, the real feat became the start once again, and yet we carried on as the sunlight shifted downward in the western sky. Just short of mile marker 64, Zach, my 7-year-old son, took off with us on a planned run the last 2.7 miles of lap four. The going was slow. In the midst of skipping and hopping, a root caught him and he hit the dirt. Sheepishly, he arose to the words of his Uncle Mike, who declared that he was now a real ultra-marathoner. He was my son. As we came to shores of the lake, light was rapidly retreating. Emma and Matthew hopped on for the last quarter of a mile as we ran among the smiles of curious onlookers and families and friends in support. The cameras flashed. Suddenly, I had an escort of the most youthful kind when my body felt anything but. Zach would declare days later that his ankle was still recovering. His beaming smile of trail lore would betray the ache he professed.

I came in search of a hundred miles. I never made it. I decided that I had long since got what I had come for. Yet I wondered what the darkness would have held. I wondered if I would regret the decision later. But now was not the time to think of then, or what may have been. Now, was the time to say thanks, and be done. Now was the time to let the mystery of later be. It was time to go home.

† † † †

Just a couple of years before this race, even after completing an Ironman in 2011, the thought of a hundred mile race by foot would have seemed preposterous to me. Even the year before, when I was preparing for the 50 mile trail run, I doubted whether my body, better equipped for sports designed for a larger build, would withstand the endurance and strength needed to complete even 50 miles. But small pieces began to fall into place. Years before while living in St. Louis, I sensed that in order to remain healthy and forego commonly used medications for blood pressure and cholesterol, I would have to find a way to convert my body from what was previously intended to play football and basketball to one that designed for more endurance activities. Like many of us (although some do well), it becomes more difficult to rally and plan regular team activities, not to mention that our bodies become less equipped to handle sports like basketball, football, and the like as we get older. There are many reasons that an NFL player's average career last 3 years, even beyond the brutal toll that all the contact takes. Most professional athletes are long past their prime when they hit their early to mid 30's.

But while most athletes are long done or just hanging on by their mid 30's, many endurance athletes are just reaching their prime, and continue on for long after. Mark Allen won his 6th and final Ironman World Championship in Kona at the age of 37. Recently, Nina Kraft became the oldest female to win an Ironman (Louisville) at the age of 46. Yiannis Kouros set the six day running record of an astounding 643 miles at 49 year of age. George Sheehan mentioned earlier ran his personal best Boston Marathon, in a stellar 3 hours, 1 minute, at the youthful age of 61.

But for most people like me, when we enter are twenties, we are faced with a *question*. Just how are you going to embrace your physicality for the next 50-60 years or more of your life? Whether we realize it or not, we gradually come to an agreement with ourselves. We are either going to use one or varied ways of maintaining and strengthening the body that God has given us, or we are going to rely more on what science and medicine has to offer. Although there are a few people that seem to get away with moving little and yet remaining independently healthy (and of course, everyone likes an exception that allow for an easier route), the large majority of people must come to grips with this question by the time their frontal lobes stop developing in the mid 20's. It is also around this time when people begin to really notice their declining metabolism. Even if you don't hear it or take it seriously, the question remains.

For those who do address this question, then there often comes a set of goals although this can coincide with the question itself. For example, some people realize the need to be healthier, and so sign up for a half-marathon to give them a clear reason to start running. Others start running to get healthy, and then suddenly start to wonder just what kind of goals might be possible. But regardless what precipitates the change, the question regarding our health, and the goals that may arise, are important for many in finding ways to at least build activity into their normal lives.

But there is another level, and this ties directly into what I mentioned earlier about health being a pursuit, not a commodity. Tim Noakes, in his book *The Lore of Running*, talks about the transition from being a jogger, to a racer, to a runner. A jogger jogs because it is good for him. A racer races because he or she desires the competition. But a runner runs because it becomes him, and he becomes it. Running becomes absorbed into a runner's inner self, and although competition and health remain important, running most notably becomes a full experience of oneself, or as I might say, a oneness with the physical body granted by Him, animated by the spiritual soul.

What becomes so powerful about this process is that many, like me, grew up hating running. In high school, it was simply a means to an end, a way to get in better shape, and for years I left it alone after the competitive sports were finished. But when I finally signed up for that first half-marathon just before our oldest kids were born, something began to speak to me deeply still a lifetime in the making just as cycling and eventually swimming provided something unique, too. I began to feel gratitude, and awe, that could sustain itself days and weeks after physical activity in a very psychological way. I began to feel a sense of camaraderie with those who took on similar challenges. Even today as I sitting here writing this, the joy of running eight miles this morning with a close friend (and his friend, who is a gifted professional triathlete) on the trails, who really inspired me to believe an ultramarathon was possible, will remain with me for some time.

For men especially, the entry of kids and busyness of a professional life can easily leave us feeling isolated at times. Although there are opportunities to bond with other men, most of these do focus around sedentary, or rather relaxing activities. I am not demeaning these activities, as they can be great, healthy ways of bonding and even give back to others and the community, as many of our local groups do. But there is a reality that cannot be sidestepped. Many of them utilize activities, such as eating fatty foods, drinking, gambling, smoking, etc.... that are not healthy as described prior in the discussion of outlets and inlets. But in order to seek out bonding and camaraderie, many men find themselves involved in these groups, and by default (or desire) engage in the unhealthy practices. In the process, even as attempts are made towards greater spirituality and social engagement, our physicality (and sometimes psychology) suffers. Think even of the last religious retreat you attended. Just how much unhealthy food and sedentary time was made available that none of us really needed?

It is at this point that the trail and roadways and waterways offer a unique opportunity to forge a bond, both interpersonally and intrapersonally. These are certainly not the only ways this can occur, but when two or more people come together under a situation of physical demand, a unique interaction takes place. It really can be an intersection of the four dimensions, as the body is engaged, the mind is acute, the relationships are raw, and the spirit resides in full animation. Like any experience, it is not as if we are lifted into a cloud of transcendence and love. But it as if we are putting effort into something that is so primal, so deeply imbedded into our being, that we can start to feel like the little children Christ calls us to be. As quoted in Matthew 18:3: "Truly I say to you, unless you are converted and become like children, you will not enter the kingdom of heaven."

Which is exactly what my wife said to me today when she came back after running laps on a nearby grassy hill for the first time. She described the joy in jumping over a little rivulet each time she crossed its path. She felt like a "little kid" even as she would return home to assume the challenges and joy that came with being a married, mother of six. It is what I feel at the indescribable joy of pushing really hard up my favorite hills in the woods, or engaging on a particular section of road on bike or afoot. All pretenses about who you are fall to the ground, and you find yourself so engaged in the process for that particular time, other concerns really do dissipate into the atmosphere. Although it can take years for a person to sense this (and some never claim these feelings), I do believe that childish joy is there for all of us, even if it comes from a simple walk in the fading sun or striding into the frosty sunrise. There is a renewal of the relationship with ourselves, and the world where we have been placed.

Activity of any kind can offer this, but we cannot force these experiences to occur. We can only be responsible for the effort that it takes to allow for these possibilities, and the acceptance that a body fully engaged can give rise to harmony and peace not realized before.

10

We Are What We Eat

One cannot think well, love well, sleep well, if one has not dined
well.
                                                —Virginia Woolf

In 1886, long before fast food outlets would
become a mainstay of American culture, a little known
druggist by the name of John Pemberton used extracts of
cocoa leaves and kola nuts, sugar, and a few other
ingredients to produce a syrup. He had hoped it would be
a cure for headaches. After the business was sold to Willis
Venable due to Pemberton's failing health, it was
discovered that combining the syrup with soda water
made for a refreshing drink. Coca-Cola had emerged. By
1900, revenues topped 400,000 dollars annually. Those in
charge quickly realized that advertising was the key, and
they began to invest over 25% of their annual budget on
marketing their newfound delight. Around the same time,
thousands of miles away, the Pepsi-Cola company was
finding its way. By 1939, Pepsi-Cola's net earnings would
rise to over 5.5 million dollars.

As soda companies continued their epic rise, the
fast food world was quickly growing from its early ascent
in the Roaring Twenties. As more people owned
automobiles, the idea of going out for a "quick bite"
became increasingly appealing and feasible. The 1950's
expansion of the highway system made urban flight
possible, and restaurants began to pop up in new
suburban communities. Once the "baby boom" became a

reality post World War II, it seemed there was no stopping this new version of the American dream. In a culture where speed and efficiency were idolized, it was a match made in heaven. Not only did the culture support the trend, but the trend gradually became part of the culture. McDonald and other companies quickly realized that it wasn't just the affordable and convenient food that would sell it all, but the entire experience. Children learned to love the meal that made them feel "happy" even before they clambered over the playground just out the door. Ads taught them that the soft drinks and fast food they coveted made them attractive, young, cutting-edge, and athletic, even if the end result fell far short. Studies[1] showed that children felt fries tasted better in a McDonald's wrapper than a plain container, even if they remained unknowingly the same. Even the side of the Styrofoam cups had phrases that padded egos, congratulating you on the sophistication and charm that led you to them and just much love was being consumed.

Like soft drinks, the key to success was in the advertising. McDonald's would eventually come to spend 1.4 billion dollars annually on marketing its products. Today, there are over 8,000 restaurants in 101 countries. The McDonald's in Moscow's Red Square became the largest of its kind when it was built. Police were called in for crowd control after the opening of a restaurant in Minsk led to a mad rush of 4,000 Belarusians hungry for a taste of Americana. Worldwide sales eventually topped 32 billion dollars a year, 15 billion coming from sales outside the United States. Three new McDonald's restaurants open somewhere every day. Although each retains the iconic McDonald's identity, they also cater to the local market, serving vegetarian burgers in Holland, tatsuta chicken sandwiches in Japan, and wine in France. Their cleanliness and family friendly atmosphere are seen as a respite for some, a bane of American imperialism by others.

As the insatiable desire of more for less continued, Americans began spending a smaller percentage of their annual income on food (adjusted for inflation) than previous generations. As noted in the book, *Omnivore's Dilemma* by Michael Pollan, Americans today spend less than ten percent of their disposable income on food – less than any other group in history. The French spend approximately twenty percent, the Chinese fifty percent. Americans also spend less time preparing it – a meager thirty-one minutes a day on average, including clean-up. While the cost of fresh fruits and vegetables has climbed above the Consumer-price index, carbonated drinks and sugar and sweets showed the opposite trend, becoming cheaper than ever before. Americans began consuming more and moving less, defying the immutable laws of the calorie cycle. Soft drinks stopped becoming a special treat, instead turning into a daily staple. As more than half of all children consumed soft drinks daily (and almost ¾ of all boys), youth and adults were finding out this habit was leading them to much more than a tasty indulgence. Studies began to show that a soft drink a day was a 10+ pound a year habit. Estimates are that youth currently drink carbonated beverages at a 2:1 ratio compared to milk. Soda sales per person went from 40 gallons per year in 1985 to 53 gallons in 2000.

Once our special treats became our daily eats, we realized that we were no longer limited by the size of our ceramic plate. Bagels that just twenty years ago averaged three inches in diameter became six inches. French fries that were once 2.4 ounces per portion skyrocketed to 6.9 ounces[2]. And sodas that were 6.5 ounces more than tripled to twenty ounces. Just in these three food items we had suddenly picked up almost 800 more calories, with dinner yet to be served[3]. All the while, our sluggish trend continued, not just because of the food that was weighing us down, but because of all the wonderful conveniences that made our lives so much easier.

But somewhere along the way, this American dream began to sizzle, only to eventually burst into flames. The rates of overweight teens began to triple. Over sixty percent of adults were labeled as overweight, with almost ¾ of males attaining this dubious distinction. Type 2 diabetes rates soared, threatening (along with other factors) to make the generation born after 2000 the first one since the Civil War to have a shorter life expectancy than their parents. Obesity will soon overtake smoking as the leading cause of death. As noted earlier, being overweight has become the "new normal." The sale of oversized coffins became a very profitable business. Experts predict that unless the obesity crisis is halted, our health care system will collapse under the weight of its own excess.

And so once again, we are left with a harsh reality. What seems too good to be true, has in fact, been even worse than we would have predicted. We have become our own worst enemies in ways that profitable companies had known we would. Although we attempt to rationalize and try to make ourselves feel better about the new "healthy" choices we are making, it turns out that "low fat" or "non-fat" is a lot more fat than we need after all. Worst of all, our kids have bought into the same dream. It is the kind of dream brilliantly advertised recently by the king of sodas. Its commercial told of a tale where one young guy, fresh out of school with no experience, could have it all – money, happiness, big toys, unattached beautiful women at his beck and call, stocks/bonds, promotions – all perfectly captured by the zero-calorie, delicious, refreshing drink that carries seemingly no price at all.

The lie continues on...but are we and our youth even aware?

† † † †

It is a peculiar time in the world of food production and consumption. Just as the obesity crisis has been well-documented, and the proliferation of non-nutritious, artificial foods continue, we have never had more access to healthy options than we do now. Although concerns continue to be voiced about hormonal use, pesticides, and genetic engineering, the reality is that natural foods, of all different kinds and origins, are becoming more and more available, even in discount groceries stores. Not that long ago, consumers were either limited by seasonal availability, regional options, and more difficulty with transport. But today, I can find quinoa at the nearby discount stores and fresh fruits and vegetables of many varieties almost anywhere.

Many people bemoan that eating healthier is more expensive, especially when raising a larger family. To some extent as noted in the prior paragraphs, this is true. But what also is true is that we are spending less and less of our disposable income on food, which suggests that we are assigning less value to what we eat[4]. When the options are between a high-calorie frozen pizza for three dollars, and more natural ingredients that will run us twice that much for dinner, once again it seems that we place a higher value on economics and taste buds than what more natural foods can do for us, now and ongoing.

The issue of assigning value to food based on a strictly economic comparison also belies the idea that evidence clearly shows that more natural, unprocessed foods improve many health factors, including immunity. If we are simply to stay with an economic comparison, then at the very least, we must factor in just how the pursuit of a healthy diet likely decreases doctor visits and medication usage over the lifetime. Not only would this suggest that a long-term economic view of food is more complicated than comparing the price of frozen pizza to produce, but with improved health likely comes improved relationships and decreased psychological difficulties. No one denies that food/beverages and mood are strongly connected, both in regards to elevation and depression. We know that the link between obesity and mental health is strong, even in our young kids[5]. Recent evidence indicates that regular consumption of soft drinks and junk food are connected to increased behavioral and attention problems.

Take a simple example. A young couple enters marriage, both as fairly active people who enjoy spending time together exercising and in natural surroundings. But gradually over time, the husband starts to gain a significant amount of weight largely due to many meals eaten on the go as a salesman. Gradually, he becomes more sedentary, and although his wife tries to get him to go walk and run with her, he usually declines. Dysthymic mood and irritability increasingly set in, and when he gets home from work at night or from the week, he just wants to relax in front of the television and rarely finds himself willing to engage in alternate activities. Both individuals sense that their interests and lives are slowly changing, and although they love each other deeply, the regular intimacy that they once shared now becomes increasingly scarce.

There are many reasons that gluttony finds itself among the seven deadly sins. The most obvious is that the focus of food increasingly takes the place of other more important endeavors, most importantly the endeavor of pursuing nourishment first and foremost through Christ. Yet the transgression of gluttony is an insidious one, especially as "overweight" becomes just who we are. We can easily understand how sins such as greed and wrath can hurt other people. Gluttony, however, often seems like the "white sin" of the seven deadly sins because of its apparently benign nature. Herein lays the trap. Even as our bodies slowly expand as a direct result of our food choices, and markers such as weight, blood pressure, and cholesterol do inform us of an inner reality, there are just as serious consequences that often occur of which we rarely are privy. Our energy decreases. Our attention may wane. Our mental acuity is threatened. Our irritability often heightens. But rarely are there concrete markers to show us just how much has changed.

But there is a bigger issue at hand that does not place the accountability in our hands, or that of advertisers and food distributers. It has been labeled as the elephant in the Church, and it has left us in an uncomfortable situation.   I found myself right in the middle of it one day during a sermon in which the homilist bragged about his love of buffets, and the importance of being "well fed" just as he grabbed his generous gut in a full display. I wondered. What would have been the reaction in the congregation if this same homilist (who was rightly a highly respected member of the community) had bragged about his lustful transgressions or his greedy pursuits? I suspect the reception would have looked dramatically different, and an uproar would (hopefully) have been heard on many fronts.

Even more than the state of country, the state of our Christian body of Christ, both for clergy and laity, is concerning. Over-indulging in food is especially surprising because clear teachings exist to the contrary. Here's what the Catechism of the Catholic Church has to say:

> Vices can be classified according to the virtues they oppose, or also be linked to the capital sins which Christian experience has distinguished, following St. John Cassian and St. Gregory the Great. They are called "capital" because they engender other sins, other vices. They are pride, avarice, envy, wrath, lust, gluttony, and sloth or acedia. *(no. 1866)*

And here's an admonition from Proverbs (2:19-21):

> Hear, my son, and be wise, and guide your heart in the right way. Do not join with wine bibbers,
> nor with those who glut themselves on meat. For drunkards and gluttons come to poverty,
> and lazing about clothes one in rags.

But it seems we've forgotten these and have not only accepted the secular trend that has made overweight the "new normal," we are wallowing in it. In our diocese, like many others, our fundraisers and gatherings feature the sale and consumption of very unhealthy, cheap, highly-processed foods. I support—as I believe the Church teaches—offering an abundance of varieties of food for special celebrations. Such events are wonderful for the community and fellowship they provide. But when unhealthy food is sold or handed out on an almost weekly basis, we are promoting poor health. These gatherings don't seem to qualify as "special celebrations" by any definition.

The largest fundraisers for most parishes in our area come from food/beverages sold at an annual street festival, summer socials, and Lenten fish fries. All support the purchase and consumption of some of the least nutritious foods that exist, and give parishioners in our diocese a sense that every weekend, we can support our churches through the patronage of these events.

At the risk of sounding curmudgeonly, the fish fries, which are supposed to encourage Catholics to follow their Lenten observances, undermine the spirit of Lenten fasting. Sure, we're all eating fish instead of meat, but how can a 1,500-2,000 calorie meal featuring fried fish and succulent desserts be considered in any way penitential? Fasting, done properly and responsibly, carries significant spiritual and physical benefits as noted prior. If fasting, almsgiving, and prayer are the three pillars of Lent, it seems that any table from which we seek our daily bread must have three sturdy legs (not just two), to support our pursuit of the resurrected Christ, and not only during Lent.

With each struggle, comes an opportunity, and with an opportunity can come a movement. The movement, however, starts with the person in the mirror. I believe that each of us are being challenged to truly reconsider how our food choices, both in type and quantity, are not just a physical and social undertaking, but also a psychological and spiritual one. As a people who have long been reminded (or should have been) of the dangers of gluttony, I believe we are in a good position to lead a countercultural, universal change to a deeper spirituality through better health. In doing so, and increasing our capacity to take on each uniquely divine call, we are closer to becoming, as Matthew Kelly notes, "the best version of ourselves."

If we are being honest, though, there is an intrinsic stubbornness that resists this idea of looking at food as a spiritual and psychological endeavor. It's just food, right? For some people, it is because they grew up with very little food, and now that they have worked hard to earn a more comfortable existence, they feel it is their right to drink and eat what they want, at least to a "reasonable degree." For some, it is really hard to understand how what lies on our plate can make that much of a difference in many areas of our lives. Others simply get tired of hearing the glum news about food issues, and honestly just don't like "being told" what they should and shouldn't eat. Many times over the years I have heard people begrudgingly utter the phrase "my doctor told me I have to start eating healthier and cut back on the sweets and potato chips." There is an irony to these statements. They are often accompanied by a not so subtle undertone that conveys a sense that the doctor "telling the person to do something that is not fun or reasonable" as opposed to working with him or her to make what might be a life-saving change. Many of these same people, however, would not question a mechanic's advice that all fluids put into an automobile, including, gasoline, oil, antifreeze, and brake fluid, be of high-quality so that the vehicle will run well. Why would we all not believe that a similar principle applies to the fuel that our body uses?

But this response to food changes is initiated for many different reasons. It is that these changes are perceived as not fun, and are purely done out of obligation. Both of these responses must shift dramatically in order for a revolution to occur in the world of food. We must first come to understand, as many books today actually espouse, that looking at food in a constructive, useful way, and being interested in potential new food choices, can be enjoyable and uniting. Although some people are either born with, or acquired (early in life) taste buds that do not respond as well to natural foods, it is clear that through repeated introductions to new foods (or those previously not liked), taste preferences can and do change. It can't change, though, if we stubbornly refuse options that are available, and it won't change if we only see food for what it brings to us when it still resides in our mouths.

All of this means more than what your taste buds tell you. This means more than what your heart and lungs and liver need to function well. This means more than how much energy you have, and just what your moods are going to be. This means more than how you relate to other people, and just how long you are likely to be able to play on the floor with your grandchildren and walk and run with your grown children.

Food choices *can* mean differences in all of these things. But ultimately they may also reflect the desires and goals that we embrace in our life as a whole. At times, we all need to splurge and eat something, in celebration and in relief and in pleasure. But when our daily choice of food reflect values of immediate gratification, hedonism, and inflexibility, food becomes one more way in which we defy the divine pleasures with which we have been granted. Like all the other gifts that we have been given, it seems that food was intended to be used for sustenance, development, enhancement, and even at times for pleasure, but certainly not an agent of erosion, resignation, and ultimately demise. If there is truth to the adage of "we are what we eat", then it rightly seems that what we eat echoes largely of who we are, and who we want to be.

11

There's More to Sleep than Shuts the Eye

It is a common experience that a problem difficult at night is resolved in the morning after the committee of sleep has worked on it.   —John Steinbeck

Every day for most people, something mysterious begins to take shape that still defies scientists in these times. Although the primary reasons for most basic bodily functions, such as eating and moving, have been known for centuries, sleep, or also known as slumbering or snoozing or napping or crashing, still remains an enigma in many ways. Yet, there is no single activity that we do more in our life. It is largely controlled by two bodily systems and one earthly one. One, the circadian rhythms and sleep/wake homeostasis of our body, tells us that the longer it has been since we slept, the more it is time to close our eyes. And two, the less light that we perceive, the more our brain (largely through the use of melatonin) tells us it is time for bed. The average person will sleep for 25 years in their lifetime. Infant sleep typically averages between 14-15 hours a night. Toddlers spend half of their day horizontal. Even by the time our kids reach school age, we hope that their daily hours of sleep reaches double digits.

Although researchers acknowledge that there is much to learn, what we do know increasingly sends one clear message. Sleep is vastly more than simply rest and quietness. It makes sense. Why would the human body spend a 1/3 of its time doing something unnecessary? In 2013, an article was published in the journal of Scientific American entitled, "Sleeps Role in Obesity, Schizophrenia, Diabetes...Everything." In it, the authors provide an overview of the growing mountain of studies that point to the amazing potential, and significant risks, associated with different sleep patterns. Studies have long shown that roughly 90% of people diagnosed with anxiety disorders report sleep-reported problems, the latter potentially causing or worsening the former[1]. We know that ADHD rates are higher in kids with poor sleep. We know that psychologically healthy kids look a lot like those diagnosed with ADHD when they are chronically sleep deprived[2]. If you take kids with obstructive sleep apnea and ADHD symptoms and remove their tonsils and adenoids, the improvement in attention is typically much better than using medication[3]. Shortened sleep duration in young kids is associated with a lifelong risk for obesity[4]. Long-term sleep deprivation mimics psychosis in healthy individuals[5]. If you have sleep apnea, your risk for depression is fivefold; if you have depression, the risk of apnea is fourfold.

But sleep is not just about warding off disease and disability. Good sleep is associated with learning better and remembering more. It appears that our memory is better if we "sleep on it." Taking naps after learning tasks results in greater recollection and retrieval than staying awake. Dreams, long the source of so many conjectures and theories, appear to not necessarily recreate what actually has happened, but create scenarios about events and tasks that likely serves many purposes[6]. All of us, including athletes, (especially those in intense, ongoing training) often depend on sleep, including recovery naps, to repair the body. Exercise often improves sleep. Sleep often improves exercise. Roughly two-thirds of our growth hormone, which is involved with muscle development, is secreted during sleep. Sleep helps control when we feel full, and when it is time to eat in order to prepare for the day. Sleep appears to regulate our blood sugar[7]. Studies suggest that going to bed earlier can help make a diet more successful. Even the types of foods and drinks we consume can significantly affect our sleep.

As we get deeper into the mystery, we know that not all sleep is created alike. There are stages of sleep, and patterns of sleep. Very simplistically, there are five primary stages of sleep—stages 1-4 and the Rapid Eye Movement (REM) phase. Stages 3 and 4 are considered deep, slow-wave sleep. The average child gets most of his deep sleep in the first three hours of the night (which diminishes as we get older). That is when issues, such as sleepwalking and sleep terrors, usually occur. Kids really aren't awake when this happens and therefore, can't remember a thing the next morning. On the contrary, REM sleep, usually occurs for children after the 3rd hour and increases as the night goes on. This is when nightmares typically arise, which may wake the child up and leave memories in the morning. And somewhere in the night, we all have a "point of singularity", which nearly coincides with where our body temperature reaches its nadir. At this juncture, our core temperature begins to rise, cortisol secretion increases, and the proportion of REM sleep grows. Unbeknown to us, it is as if our body begins to prepare for another day.

For many, the science of sleep might be liable to, well, put them to sleep. But the further into the spindles we get, the more astounding and captivating it becomes.

As Dr. Ruben Naimen noted in her book, *Hush: A Book of Bedtime Contemplations*, sleep becomes less about something we do, and more about who we are and the rhythms that we feel. It seems there is a psychophysiological, meta-physical, even spiritual nature to it all. Yet unfortunately, sleep appears to have become one more marketed commodity. In past two decades, artificial sleep aids have sharply risen[8]. Market research between 1998-2006 indicated sleep aid prescriptions for young adults (ages 18-24) had tripled[9]. They come by many names, on and off label, prescription and over-the-counter, medication and supplement. But all concoctions used are intended to onset or enhance sleep, or completely sedate the people who use them. Meanwhile, many researchers suggest that 80-90% of sleep difficulties could be addressed through cognitive, behavioral, and lifestyle changes. In 2014, the American Academy of Sleep Medicine (AASM) weighed in on this discussion through a document entitled Five Things Physicians and Patients Should Question. Advice #2: *Avoid use of hypnotics as primary therapy for chronic insomnia in adults; instead offer cognitive-behavioral therapy, and reserve medication for adjunctive treatment when necessary.* Advice #3: *Don't prescribe medication to treat childhood insomnia, which usually arises from parent-child interactions and responds to behavioral intervention.*

The great irony is that despite all our attempts to augment sleep, we are slumbering less than we did just a century before. Twenty percent less[10]. There are many arguments why. Maybe our biological systems are evolving. Maybe our 24/7 culture and the lure of incessant media and bright lights, whether of a mobile screen or the conventional tube, are just too alluring.

Schroeder

Maybe we think we can "beat the system" and get by just fine without adhering to time-honored needs. Years ago, I got to know a father who swore he didn't need any more than 4-5 hours of sleep a night. He was forty pounds overweight, anxious, irritable, divorced, and felt his only child was slowly parting from him. I challenged his assumptions about his need for sleep, and mused with him what just a couple of more hours a night could do for his quality of life. I am not sure if he ever saw how more darkness could lead to more light.

And maybe, just maybe, we simply don't value sleep like we do so many other things. I cringed a few years ago when I read a blog written by someone about how to truly be a successful professional. One of the messages was simple: get used to living with less sleep. It seemed like a falsity laden with strong undertones that went well beyond the zzz's. It echoed of a message we hear elsewhere, which proclaims that whatever we could find outside of ourselves—money, status, power—is well worth sacrificing what we can find within. Of course, what he forgot to mention was that even if the false promise was true (which it is not), it is only plausible for the few that could make it as he aspired. Sleep, on the other hand, is given to everyone, even though for some it seems like a nightmare, not a remedy. As a father, I never knew just how much I loved my sleep until my first kids were born. There are times when sleep might just be the most important and productive part of my day.

It is time to reclaim the value of the Betty White party, or counting our sheep, and just getting some old-fashioned shut eye. It is time to stare down the screen and let it know that the bed is calling. I think we would all be happier, and really not miss a thing. Better yet, I (and many others) think that when the demands of the day do come calling, striving for optimal sleep will only allow us to be more productive, healthier, more patient, and more loving than before. And it could all be free.

† † † †

As we reach the third pillar of health, it often comes to us as an afterthought of the first two. Although sleep periodically shows up in the headlines and certainly is central in discussions of young parents who are just learning how different life can be without sleep, its enigmatic and innocuous form (despite what we are learning) tends to relegate it to a second class citizen.

It is not only much of the general public that feels this way. Sadly, I first must admit that my training in sleep was minimal at best until I took on a role in a sleep clinic at a pediatric hospital. Discussion of sleep was almost non-existent in graduate school. It was only at the hospital that I began to acquire much more knowledge from other specialties, such as neurology, pulmonology, and the sleep specialists themselves in addition to my own seeking. My pediatric colleagues in medicine apparently feel the same way. In a survey published by Mindell & Owens, it was found that 20-40% of pediatricians and family physicians did not screen for sleep issues in a well-child visit, which is pretty amazing given that toddlers are supposed to sleep half of their day[12]. I hate to say it, but I would believe that these numbers are similar for psychologists and psychiatrists.

It seems our attitudes towards sleep, and the environment in which we snooze, often reflects our attitudes towards our daytime activities. Many people who have televisions in their bedrooms also have televisions in other parts of their homes other than usual entertainment zones, such as the living room and family room. Screens may routinely be found in kitchens, bathrooms, and certainly now in cars as most new vehicles are built with DVD players. Those who often relegate sleep to a second class status often express similar views about the foods they eat and the level of activity they endorse. This is not always the case. Yet many view the three pillars of health in a similar way—one in which health practices themselves are regarded with complacency or even derision, but certainly not as sources of enjoyment, facilitation, and even fulfillment.

There is a mysterious nature to all areas of our health, and in some ways it tests our faith more than many elements of our lives. When you really begin to ponder what happens when we eat, and how calories and nutrients and vitamins are transformed into energy, tissue, and chemicals of all sorts that sustain us for decades, it is hard not to be amazed by the process. When physical activity is morphed into new tissue and bone marrow, it is equally enigmatic about how all this occurs. But maybe sleep is the most baffling of the three. How is doing nothing so connected to growth, rejuvenation, and even the ever mystifying state of dreams, where stories are told in infinite ways?

Long the source of speculation, dreams show up in the Bible both as sources of phenomenal foreshadowings and serious warnings. They appear as early as the story of Abraham, when God assures Abraham that he will have a son and govern many nations. God asked Solomon what he wanted in a dream, and he asked for "wisdom." Dreams were used to assure the fathers of John the

Baptist and Jesus that their sons were to come, and to trust God in the mystery of how all this would occur. Dreams warned Joseph to take a different path in avoiding the wrath of Herod. Even Pilate's wife had a nightmare that told her Jesus was innocent, and should be freed.

From the bible to psychoanalysis, dreams became a source of divine intercession to repressed memories and conflicts. Interpretation of dreams became a reputed way of seeing into the inner psyche, and volumes were, and continue to be, written about the ways in which dreams give us insight into the unconscious. Although some still adhere to these ideas, most researchers of today have come to believe that dreams are the brains way of sorting through information, and consolidating what we need and thinning what we don't.

Yet regardless of what one thinks, it appears that dreams may be the pinnacle of the mystery of modern health. As humans go in search of more and more in the materialistic world, it is worth pausing for a moment and considering just how improbable it is that our bodies and minds can function the way they can. It is reasonable to be in awe of man-made wonders, of skyscrapers that rise, of roller coasters that invert, of planes that can fly. Each of them are remarkable in what they can do and how stately they appear. But consider this. One single human body can think, speak, run, jump, draw, write, paint, taste, sing, see, hear, feel, smell, cry, add, subtract, laugh, remember, recall, grow, heat, cool, sleep, excrete, consume, digest, regenerate, and immunize. These are the simplest things we do. Most accomplish all these tasks by the age of six. Most of these functions happen by the age of two.

As we close our focus on the pillars of health, it bears reminding that wholeness of one's bodily self is an opportunity given to all of us. Even those afflicted by various illnesses and maladies can come to understand what it means to pursue a pure measure of health. Recently, I spoke to a friend who indicated that she had been diagnosed with Multiple Sclerosis (MS) during the past year. Despite struggling with this news, she expressed solace and optimism in that a sustained diet change had left her feeling better than even before this diagnosis had occurred. Although worried about what would come, there was a measure of joy that there were things given to her that could better her situation.

This may not always seem to be the case. Yet having been around, and heard so many stories of people pursing better health in situations marred by physical heartache and affliction, what if the pursuit of health, even of the most miniscule kind, is synonymous with a particular pursuit of joy. We all know that we feel better when we feel healthier. It only takes a bout of the flu or a broken leg to remind us just how much of a "gift" our health is, certainly not something that we deserve or can believe we are the architect for. But as with pride, it is imperfect effort that we can own, and must own, if the holiness is to emerge from the pursuit of bodily wholeness. Once effort interacts with this amazing, mysterious gift, it will seem impossible that we will not find ourselves in a spiritual wonderland every time our heart rate rises and our body engages in a vigorous quest for what opens the doors to the unique callings with which we have been given.

The Social Dimension

Let the words of my mouth and the meditation of my heart be acceptable in your sight, O Lord, my rock and redeemer.

Psalm 19:14

12

Partner Bill of Rights

Courage means to keep working a relationship, to continue seeking solutions to difficult problems, and to stay focused during stressful periods.

—Denis Waitley

In 1993, the World Health Bank estimated that domestic violence, or intimate partner violence (IPV), was a greater cause of poor health than traffic accidents and malaria combined[1]. It was believed that 5-20% of healthy years lost for women were attributed to IPV[2]. By definition, violence is considered to be any physical, verbal, or sexual assault that significantly comprises a person's body, trust, and sense of self[2]. But it is not solely a female issue even as women are disproportionately perpetrated against in this way.

Results from a study conducted in the United States found that 22.1 percent of women and 7.4 percent of men reported acts of IPV in their lifetime[3]. Over fifty percent of those surveyed claimed to be physically assaulted at some point in their life, often as children. Certain groups appear more at risk even beyond the obvious female preponderance. For example, one report indicated that women in rural or isolated areas noted significantly higher rates of abuse than those in urban areas[4]. According to the Center for Disease Control (CDC), estimates are that one-half of all stalkings, one-fourth of all physical assaults, and one-fifth of all rapes are reported to authorities[5]. It suggests that substantiated, or even alleged abuse, only represents the tip of the iceberg.

The cost of abuse to societies and the individuals is tremendous, none more than in the area of psychological health. Fear, anxiety, mistrust, depression, fear of intimacy and other consequences often persist long after the threat of physical violence is gone. But those who know this area well will attest that the issue is much more complex than what the abuser brings. Intimate partner violence often develops in insidious ways and through seemingly isolated circumstances, only to emerge as a cycle that looks all too similar no matter what story is told. Tension, rage, blaming, protection, denial, reconciliation, and calm underlay a process by which each incident becomes part of a larger cycle. Beneath this, one area common to abuse is each partner's difficulty in clearly communicating not only the expectations of the relationship, but the consequences (intended and unintended) that stem from an erosion of basic, human rights.

To initiate change, we must bring a voice to the basic expectations of a relationship, and what will occur if these expectations are not met. This is especially important for our young people as they learn how to navigate the challenges and promises of intimacy. The goal is to assist them in developing the necessary skills for personal relationships. These expectations are defined in the following Partner Bill of Rights. To some, this may seem very obvious and easily achievable; to others, it may seem like an unattainable request. But for all, it speaks to an inner reality of our longing to be treated in a way that we deserve by those who promise to love us the most.

I have the right to be treated as a human being, equal in worth even though different in roles. When I feel disrespected or made to feel stupid, I have the right to be heard about the way I feel dehumanized. If I continue to be treated poorly, I have the right to seek out advice and counsel as needed.

I have the right to be treated as an adult, not as a child. As an adult, I have the right to make decisions about what I can handle, and information should not be withheld from me on the premise that I am not strong enough to handle it. I will make that decision.

I have the right to feel safe in my relationship. If you do anything that violates my security, or I feel threatened in any way, understand that I have the right to seek safety for myself and my children with those I trust.

I have the right to coherent conversations and coherent answers. If you say something to me that does not make logical sense, I have the right to ask questions until I feel that a reasonable, sensible answer is given. If you are not able to provide coherent answers, understand that I will seek out counsel and advice from close friends or families that may be able to.

I have the right to ask any question about your actions or behaviors at any time. Although you are not bound to share all of your thoughts, temptations, or other odd or uncomfortable ideas, you, as my significant other, are bound to share what you did and why it occurred. If you do not give satisfactory answers, I have the right to continue to ask until answers are provided, even if you are annoyed by the questions as they occur. If satisfactory answers are not provided, know that I will not be able to trust you as long as they are not, even if I work to forgive you for what I know.

I have the right to share my insecurities, worries, or concerns at any time, even if it involves something that occurred in the past. Although I promise to try and not flood you with these, and work to resolve my own struggles and those around past issues, I have the right to let you know when I am feeling unsure or uncertain about the status of our relationship. If you disregard or scoff at these concerns, I have the right to bring them up again until I feel that you adequately understand me.

I have the right to not be blamed or "pulled through the mud" for mistakes that you have made. Although I am willing to hear about areas in which I may have contributed to the problems we have, I have the right to not be attacked or shamed for the errors of your ways. I do not deserve to be the scapegoat for your sins.

I have the right to apologies when you make mistakes just as I should continually seek out forgiveness from you when I go wrong in my ways. When you do not apologize for your mistakes or outrage, understand that I will naturally feel bitter and that although I may not like this in myself, I will feel less likely to want to apologize as well for my wrongs.

I have the right to suggest ideas about things I feel are important even as I work hard not to badger, demand, or nag at you. If you do not listen to me, I have the right to bring these suggestions back to you until you entertain a reasonable response or consideration to them.

I have the right to clear, regular, daily communication about all types of issues. Although you may not think that I understand much about what you do, I nonetheless have the right to hear about things that go on in all aspects of your life whether or not you feel it matters.

I have the right to chastity in our relationship. If you violate this commitment, know that it hurts me deeply and leaves me feeling that I have not provided for you in the way that I should have, and that something is wrong with me. Do not expect that I will be able to resolve this hurt and pain for some time. I have the right, in a respectful way, to express and discuss my feelings with you in this matter, even as I work to forgive you.

I have the right to demand that in the "contract of our marriage," this bond supersedes the contract or code of any other type of relationship, family or friend. "Guy codes" or "girl codes" do not trump "spousal codes." If this happens, it will lead me to trust you less.

Finally, I have the right to a relationship that promotes the health of each other, our children, and our united body. If you do anything to jeopardize the health of these three most important gifts, then I have the right to do what I need to do to make sure that this is resolved, even if it involves taking drastic steps. I have the right to protect and shield our children from harm, and ultimately, I have the right and responsibility to make sure that my issues, your issues, and our issues do not leave the next generation in a worse place, now and forever.

And if we are married, please know that I committed to you for life, in richer and poorer, in sickness and in health, and in good and in bad. I take that commitment more seriously than any other commitment I have made in my life. In making that commitment, I committed my life to you so that we would both grow (for us and our children), not be degraded, dehumanized, or disregarded. Because of this, I promise to you that if you violate the spousal rights of our marriage, I will not accept these terms nor should we accept them together. I do this not out of pride or malice, but out of love because each of us promised to another, in the presence of others, to be unified in our search for a transcendent life regardless of the trials or tribulations that come along the way.

† † † †

"Teacher, which is the great commandment in the Law?" And He said to him, 'YOU SHALL LOVE THE LORD YOUR GOD WITH ALL YOUR HEART, AND WITH ALL YOUR SOUL, AND WITH ALL YOUR MIND.' This is the great and foremost commandment. The second is like it, 'YOU SHALL LOVE YOUR NEIGHBOR AS YOURSELF.' On these two commandments depend the whole Law and the Prophets" (Matthew 22: 36-40).

We begin with a simple, yet undeniable premise. When Jesus was asked what the two greatest commandments were, his reply focused on one topic: relationships. The first was our relationship with God. Yet as Christ tells us, "Truly I say to you, to the extent that you did it to one of these brothers of Mine, even the least of them, you did it to Me" (Matthew 25:40). This takes us to the second greatest commandment, even if it had never been explicitly stated. It is our relationship with others. And if this wasn't enough to make it clear just how important our relationships are when it comes to our spiritual pursuits, then we should consider the Ten Commandments. It is loaded with relationship dos and don'ts. You should honor your mother and father, love your God above all things. You shouldn't lie, steal, murder, and commit adultery.

But most of the egregious issues that result in abuse, divorce, adultery, estrangement, and murder don't start as obviously as the outcomes show. In those first few years of dating, patterns begin to emerge that often dictate just how partners will relate to each other for most of their lives. The source of these habits are many. Some people grew up with parents embroiled in domestic violence and contentious communications. Some struggled to manage stress in other areas, and those at home suffered as scapegoats for the challenges of the day. As noted in prior chapters, some began to have health and/or addiction struggles that resulted in less ability to manage frustrations and communication appropriately.

There are an infinite number of causes that result in one human being taking advantage of another. But in every instance, there is an erosion of basic human rights, and there are situations and people that enable these behaviors to occur, the seeds of which often start in seemingly benign ways.

It is tempting to relegate communication patterns as simply personal preferences, and not critical spiritual and psychological endeavors. But if we do this, we are walking the relativistic tightrope that is not supported by our theological beliefs. This is not a matter of men and women embracing different roles as determined by biology, culture, and socialized behaviors. It is easy to deny these basic partner rights on the basis of these three issues, and forego a true discussion into this matter. Yet, let us once again listen to the words of our Lord, which were radical then, and in many places and situations, are just as radical now.

"YOU SHALL LOVE THE LORD YOUR GOD WITH ALL YOUR HEART, AND WITH ALL YOUR SOUL, AND WITH ALL YOUR MIND.' This is the great and foremost commandment. The second is like it, 'YOU SHALL LOVE YOUR NEIGHBOR AS YOURSELF.' On these two commandments depend the whole Law and the Prophets." "Truly I say to you, to the extent that you did it to one of these brothers of Mine, even the least of them, you did it to Me."

When it says we should love others as yourself, there is no escape clause for biology, culture, or socialized behaviors. This should never be more evident than the way in which Christ treated women and those of other ethnicities, classes, and cultures, who for many were considered second class citizens. Ask yourself this. How many times does Christ clearly elevate those of a different gender or circumstance in his direct interactions and teachings, whether in parables or direct words? As much as we should respect the culture a person was raised, and the prior experiences he or she has had, the commandments appear to give us no wiggle room when it comes to the way we treat other people. They challenge us to accept no excuses for the way in which we treat our fellow human beings, none more important than those

132

closest to us. If we do not like to be discarded, undermined, degraded, dehumanized, deceived, or offended in any other way, then behaving in this manner is certainly not loving others as we love ourselves. Even better, His commandments mandate that if we are to grow in any area, this is the area that we should grow if we are to seek out eternal salvation.

But so often, the process of how these offenses play out in a daily way becomes very convoluted, thereby suggesting a clear need for a Bill of Rights for all partner relationships, even if they do not adhere to the mandates of our Christian beliefs. This is a critical point that often gets missed in our criticism of relationships that exist. Although we may not believe that varying types of relationships and living situations that have become more common today are healthy, moral circumstances, what Christ made clear is that above all, we must first and foremost focus on the way we treat God, directly and via even "the least of them." Those who are living together may be living in sin, but according to Christ's mandate, the greatest sins, and most important areas for growth and renewal, are the ways in which each other is treated. I am not saying this to draw attention away from other transgressions, such as the sin of adultery, or suggesting that unhealthy circumstances cannot and do not set the stage for greater risk. But I am simply noting that in the midst of outrage, disdain, and politicizing of issues such as cohabitation and same-sex relationships, the way in which people are treating each other is often demoted as secondary in importance, seemingly in defiance of the commands we have been given.

That being said, there are a few basic tenets that underlie the rights that we appear called to in our relationships. But before we address these deep-seeded responsibilities, it is important to reiterate what has been discussed earlier. So often when we seek to improve our relationships with others, we forget that often the most important thing that we can do is improve ourselves first, or at least as we go along the way. If we are struggling with physical, psychological, or spiritual difficulties, it is very likely that this is going to have a serious impact on how we treat others. If we do not treat our own body as a temple, how likely is that we would see others in this way? If we do not regard our mind as a gift from God designed to think and feel in the clearest way possible, but instead abuse or do not use it daily in healthy ways, how would we expect that we would regard the psychological state of another with great care? If we look our own spiritual life as a village in ruins, or even as a trivial or unworthy matter, then how likely will it be that we take serious the spiritual needs of another?

In this way, we are called to self-love before it seems we can truly love another although sometimes the process of giving ourselves fully to another can evoke an awareness of the worth that we have. Still, often when people hear a term like self-love, it evokes a negative connotation similar to narcissism, vanity, or self-absorption. This is not the self-love of which I am speaking. Untainted self-love is consistent with the simple belief that in being created in the image and likeness of God, each of us is of indeterminable worth. It does not seek to deny or hide our sinful imperfections, but makes it clear that we all have a uniquely divine purpose. Nothing should make us feel more humble than coming to truly believe this. Nothing may be more critical in our attempts to improve our interpersonal relations than embracing this idea. Very often in the noble intent to improve our bond with those closest to us, we find ourselves stalled in the same places, with the same obstacles remaining in place. Our immediate reaction is to either assume that something is wrong with the other person, or that something is wrong with the chemistry and communication that exists between me and my significant other. Sometimes this is the case. But repeatedly, we neglect to seriously ponder a third option: we might be the biggest part of the problem. The log in our own eye may *actually* be more difficult to see than the splinter in another.

Moving beyond this critical point, though, we enter into the realm of what it really means to love another as yourself. The true scope of this topic is well beyond this book, and is certainly a subject of debate and discussion that will continue as long as the world exists. But embedded in the Bill of Rights are a few ideas that set the stage for the kind of love in which we all do desire, when we get past our pain and pretenses and pride.

The first is a sense of congruence. Congruence speaks to the idea of both being treated as an adult (not a child) and equal in worth, even if different in roles. People at times may use the term egalitarian. Although there is significant overlap, this idea of congruence does not quibble nor contend with the idea that men and women are often called to different roles even though flexibility within these roles may not only be required at times, but also be healthy for that person and the couple as a whole. To suggest that particular functions taken on by a father or mother are simply the result of socialization is to ignore a vast base of medical knowledge that demonstrates how female and male bodies are often uniquely designed for specific tasks. What congruence truly means is that each significant other is treated as a critical, whole partner and that there is not an abuse of power or authority that stems from either person.

For example, a wife should not be able to spend money whenever she wants to without recourse, but then expect that the husband check in about any major or irregular expenses that occur, even if she makes much of the money. This would not be congruent because one individual is being subjected to a different, second class expectation than the other. Situations such as these send a clear message of incongruence that ends up making the relationship appear as an arbitrary, or even unfair situation, which looks more like of a parent and a minor, not two full-functioning adults.

A second underlying principle is the idea of health and security. Both speak to physical and psychological issues that address the well-being of each individual, and thereby the couple as a whole. From a psychological sense, a good example of neglecting this principle is when a husband repeatedly unloads and blames his own stress on his wife without regard for how this affects her well-being. At times, this may even escalate to domestic violence, but this is not necessarily the case. What chronically happens, though, is that one partner uses the other as a stress reliever, and thereby disregards just how much of a negative impact this may have on the other person. Clearly, the husband would not desire the same from his wife, to be loved in this way. Yet he does not consider this perspective because he is too embroiled in his own issues. From a physical sense, a ready example is of a smoker whose significant other does not smoke, but continues on in this behavior (especially at home), despite the well-researched effects of secondhand smoke. I recognize that addictions are very difficult to break. Yet I recognize more that a true partnership puts the needs, and health, of the other before his or her own. It is one thing to endanger one's own health, but it seems quite a transgression to knowingly endanger that of a loved one.

Accountability and transparency compile the third assumption that underlies the Partner Bill of Rights. So often we hear people, including ourselves, make excuses for why they forewent a commitment they have made. Although unforeseen issues do arise at times, very often the excuses that we feel brewing inside of us are not acceptable ones. Relationships really do require a repeated relinquishing of pride and "sucking it up at times" when worse seems to overshadow better, sickness overshadows health, or poorer overshadows richer. But when we do make mistakes, or find ourselves conflicted and uncertain, transparency (or lack thereof) emerges as an undeniable key to what often allows a relationship to flourish, barely survive, or take a complete nose dive for good. If we take the route of simply saying, "I forgot about it" when we know d--n well that forgetting had nothing to do with it, we are not loving others the way we would want to be loved. If we reply with "I don't know" when we have enough thoughts and ideas to fill a book, but don't feel like discussing something, we are not loving others the way we would want to be loved.

No one wants to feel left in the dark. No one wants to feel as though their needs are secondary to the needs and wants of others. In our self-sacrifice, we may be called to repeatedly make this choice ourselves, but when others make this choice for us, it does not speak of a relationship grounded in mutual love. Being accountable and transparent is often very difficult, and the desire to avoid situations is a palpable urge that all of us know full well. But when a husband repeatedly refuses to acknowledge or explain why he leaves home for hours or more at a time, then he is not being both accountable and transparent. When this occurs, both for seemingly small and large issues, it renders the relationship as a roadway full of unpredictable detours and wrong turns instead of one as an avenue for progress.

Forgiveness is the fourth principle. As I will address more in depth later, forgiveness must be a dynamic state of being, not something that occurs just in isolated circumstances. Without a constant admission of our own imperfections and wrongdoings, in an open, honest forum, then the relationship quickly becomes a skewed semblance of a mutual commitment to the truth that it was intended to be. It turns into either a one-sided ego trip, or a repeated attempt by each person to find reasons other themselves why problems and obstacles keep suspending progress forward.

But ultimately, beneath all of these principles lies one simple idea that is anything but simple to practice on a consistent basis. It is the discipline of empathy. As defined by Dictionary.com, empathy is "the intellectual identification with or vicarious experiencing of the feelings, thoughts, or attitudes of another." It comes from the Greek root word of *path* (base of the word páschein), which means to suffer, while *em* (variant of the prefix *en*) indicates that a person is put in a particular place or circumstance. In essence, empathy denotes when someone attempts to puts him or herself in the position of another, as an honest attempt to really understand another's plight and suffering. Said another way, I empathize with someone else when I metaphorically "put myself in another person's shoes" or attempt to "see things from his or her perspective." It is different than sympathy, which means to feel sorry for another person, but can imply a sense of distance or pity, not necessarily a true attempt to meet someone where they are. And empathy directly contrasts with apathy, which indicates a callous indifference or uncaring about particular circumstances or someone's situation.

The real challenge of empathy is that in its purest form, it requires a cessation of pride and anxiety for the person attempting to be empathetic. When a spouse comes to us in frustration about a particular situation, we may often be tempted to feel as if we have addressed this issue enough, and pride fully shut down further conversations. I might also be afraid of what will happen if I allow a conversation to ensue, even if I realize that the concern or desire being put forth is a legitimate one. True empathy is so difficult because in foregoing our own prideful or anxious responses, we are attempting to clear our mind of our own pretenses and needs (at least for a brief time) and really, really be willing to internalize just how our significant other feels. Empathy does not mean that we have to squash or ignore our own needs. In fact, if a relationship is to be truly mutual and empathetic, it is absolutely necessary that both individuals in a couple be very honest about what they are thinking and feeling. But empathy does mean that we cannot have a prefabricated defense ready to go when our partner comes to us in need or uncertainty. It means we must really listen, and discern what our response and reactions would be if I was in his or her position.

If partners authentically make attempts daily to be empathetic, then many of the other needs in a healthy relationship will fall into place. If we truly love your significant other enough to try and understand their ever-changing position in life, even if it is inconvenient or uncomfortable, then chances are that wholeness will begin to emerge more and more within our relationships. Like anything else, though, the discipline of empathy only matters if we put practices in place that follow-up on what our empathetic attempts reveal. Again, for empathy to be effective, both partners must practice it consistently. If one does not, then it certainly doesn't justify one person's needs being met while the other person is left to "fend for themselves". Although certainly not with all people, it is impressive how a shift towards a consistent, empathetic perspective by one person can become infectious in the household. As Mahatma Ghandi once said, "Be the change you wish to see..." If we wish that everyone in our household would try and better meet people where they are, instead of responding with anger, accusations, and assaults of many kinds, then we must reflect whether we are modeling this very attribute. In order to love your neighbor as yourself, you must first come to know your neighbor as yourself. How can we truly love what we don't know and understand?

13

The Almighty Word

You can change the world by changing your words...Remember, death and life are in the power of the tongue.

—Joel Osteen

In 1963, Lyman Wynne and Margaret Singer introduced the concept of *communication deviance* (CD) to describe fragmented patterns of interaction that are characterized by vagueness, interrupting, lack of closure, and irrelevant comments[1]. CD frequently occurs when actions, words, and nonverbal cues regularly contradict each other and are not conducive to direct, clear communication. As the decades persisted, research increasingly indicated that youth who grew up in families where CD is the norm are more likely to exhibit later psychiatric problems, especially schizophrenic symptoms[2]. Much of the research also indicated that patterns of CD are largely stable, persisting over time and in different situations.

As the findings regarding CD emerged, so did a similar vein of research looking at *expressed emotion* (EE). Individuals and families that are high in EE frequently use hostile and critical means in giving feedback, and parents often become emotionally overinvolved in even minor matters. In combination with CD, it is found that high EE was also associated with worse outcomes in children, especially in the area of psychotic conditions.

All of us as parents engage in these patterns to a certain degree. We are not always clear and direct with what we say. Our actions do not always reflect the words we use and gestures we display. We get angry as sometimes we should. We yell when it is probably least effective, and interrupt when answers might not be far away. So as we enter into this discussion, it is critical to understand that the topic I am broaching is not meant as a condemnation of our imperfect nature as parents, but a conscientious examination of how patterns of communication in our homes make such a difference.

Let's begin with a simple point of reflection. Think back (and currently) to the ways in which your parents interacted. As a young child growing up, most of us found ourselves discerning just how we would say and do things when we had kids, and often specifically how we would go about things differently. My father was (is) a tremendous parent. But I remember distinctly growing up and thinking that one day when I have children, I wouldn't walk in from work and yell at them for their shoes being out in the foyer because there were a lot of other things I (he) should be positive about. You will have to ask my kids how well I am holding to that promise today.

Yet regardless of the promises we may make, we will find that many of the ways that our parents communicated do in fact find their way into our homes decades later. Generations after generations often speak in much the same ways. Sometimes it works well; sometimes it does not, especially if the household remains such a tense, confusing place to be. Again, all of us as parents have a right to be angry at times, and none of us ever remain perfectly clear and consistent. But if this becomes the mode of operation, then it behooves us to

142

consider whether a change is in order, and just how this can occur. Otherwise, there is a good likelihood that you will hear your children repeatedly say things to your grandchildren that in your acquired wisdom will make you cringe.

This issue also becomes particularly critical in romantic relationships and marriages. As I previously wrote in my Partner Bill of Rights, every person in a relationship is deserving of communication that does not undermine, disrespect, invalidate, or otherwise disparage him or her in a devaluing way. If you truly believe in the Golden Rule, then you inherently believe this. Just as our children will most likely learn parenting from us first, so they will also learn how to treat their partner, too. And if being deviant with our communication, and repeatedly hostile and critical is the norm, expect that it very likely will become the standard operating procedure in the next household to follow.

In taking this a step further, consider how CD and EE relate to what John Gottman calls the "Four Horseman" of marriage, which he considers to be the biggest threat to a couple's happiness and commitment. The first horseman is *criticism*, which should be differentiated from a complaint. A complaint occurs when a partner voices displeasure with something that has occurred, and almost always begins with an "I" (e.g., "I was frustrated last night when you didn't clean up while I put the kids to bed like we agreed"). A criticism (often beginning with a "you") occurs when a person is purposefully degraded or demeaned (e.g., "You are so disorganized"). A second horseman is *defensiveness*, which is not only characterized by a lack of acknowledgement when wrong has occurred, but also a direct attempt to criticize the other partner as a means of reactive blaming. The third is *stonewalling*, which is basically characterized by verbal and nonverbal disengagement, or "shutting down." This occurs when someone diverts their attention to a mobile device, book, or simply leaves the area when a criticism or complaint is given. The final horseman (and considered to be the most detrimental) is *contempt*, which occurs when a partner displays disgust about the other person. This may occur in the form of eye-rolling, biting sarcasm, mockery, name-calling, or harsh humor.

Again, at any given time, we might find ourselves falling prey to some or all of these horsemen. But when they become a pattern, the underlying framework speaks of CD and EE. Instead of directly taking on the issues at hand, these harmful patterns of communication serve to increase the level of emotion, deflect true responsibility, reduce chances of really working through a problem, and ultimately sabotage true opportunities for growth. Then, the worst part happens. Our kids watch this unveil itself, and don't have the brainpower and/or life experience to realize that this is not how it is supposed to be, especially when formation can most occur. For all that we directly say and do *for* our kids, I am increasingly convinced that what probably matters just as much is what we say and do *around* our kids.

If all of this is true, it brings us back to a realization that is not necessarily an easy one, but potentially a hopeful one. It begins with specific questions, some of which may look like these. *What would I have to do to scream and criticize less? What would I have to do to communicate more clearly and honestly? What would I have to do to be more positive? What would I have to do to admit when I am wrong or contradicting?* The questions might seem infinite, and the answers might seem elusive, but they really all involve a few time-honored principles and behaviors, of which a partial list of suggestions was presented in my series later in the book entitled "Turning Distress into Joy." What we all definitely need to make even a little progress (remembering that *any* progress is still progress) is a meaningful goal, endurance, support, time, and faith. As parents, we spend years of our lives shuttling kids to practices and events, organizing memorable experiences, and providing for their educational needs. But just how much time do we really carve out in the daily task of improving ourselves and counteracting negative patterns, which in the end might make more of a difference than anything else?

Some time ago, I sat down with a married couple. The husband had grown up where CD and EE were the norm. It wasn't until he got married, and he and his wife ventured into the world of parenthood that he realized just how awful the communication had been. For years, their marriage strained at the seams as he and his wife struggled with the unwelcomed reality carried over from his youth, and the continued reality of the in-laws that were. But as the years evolved, and he begun to see that things could be much different, and much better, his focus gradually changed. He set forth on the rocky, vulnerable road of self-improvement, and it had been (and in some ways, still was) rough even as much had improved. But as I looked at them as they held hands, and they talked with great hope and passion about their son, I could not help but think how much I admired him (and her) for the journey that they had undertaken. That for all the astounding things that people do in this world, and all the public accolades that people receive, I am becoming convinced that one of the most amazing, impactful things that occur can be in the ways we *choose* to speak, when we set forth to change the wrong that has been for the right that lies within.

† † † †

The subject of communication has always been fraught with challenges associated with personality and cultural differences. Many people understandably feel frustrated by advice that seems better suited for someone of an extraverted nature than a person who embodies introverted qualities. Psychologists and other mental health professionals are often criticized for expecting people to openly articulate their thoughts and feelings on a regular basis and in constructive fashion, when for some, just the idea of sharing at all feels unnatural and contrived.

Yet, if we take a deeper look at communication patterns as we did in the previous chapter, the ultimate goal is not necessarily to encourage greater quantity, intensity, or duration of interaction (although at times this may be necessary). In conjunction with empathy, the true goal for what we say is one of authenticity. No matter of what origin or disposition or creed or leaning of any kind, authentic communication looks very much the same. It personifies the individual through a transmission of words and gestures in a way that is so real, so palpable, it is as if a person's inner being has leapt out in a transmittable form for others to see. It may occur just in a few words, or through a longing gesture of compassion or heartfelt care. But in its purest form, authentic communication does not seek to do anything but express what the heart and soul yearns and needs to say.

It's not that what is communicated may not hurt another person, especially if the communicator is being honest. But its purpose is never to detract or degrade; it is to expose and/or illuminate what may have remained hidden or unknown until the communication occurred. Not surprisingly, authenticity was a hallmark of Christ's communication style. He often said things that were perceived as shocking or damning, but if you look closer, it becomes clear that this was not his primary purpose either. The purpose of his preaching, whether in parables or direct advice, was to authentically speak the gospel from the Truth that He knew, and the truth that He was. What people came to believe about what He said was up to them. He did not engage in criticism, contempt, stonewalling, or defensiveness. He simply engaged in the practice of empathy and authenticity, whether it took two words or two hundred. As Christ stated in John 12:49, "For I did not speak of My own initiative, but the Father Himself who sent Me has given Me a commandment as to what to say and what to speak." So it seems we are called to do.

14

Striving for the Ideal—In Others

One loving heart sets another on fire.   —St. Augustine

The crescent moon slowly emerged over the turquoise, Caribbean waters lapping against the shores of Garden Key in Dry Tortugas National Park. Just minutes earlier, the blazing sun crept below the horizon silhouetted by the Loggerhead Key lighthouse. The moon provided a soft, faint glow that guided the lonely traveler in the night and understated its powerful pull on the tides, whereas its diurnal counterpart tended to covet a bolder, outgoing role. Each necessary in their own way, one seemed happy to congregate with other celestial lights while the other— soon to rise—seemed destined to illuminate a new course.

So it is with all of us in our daily lives. Each person aspires to particular goals, outcomes, or qualities that he or she feels are part of their own unique calling. It is what psychologists often describe as the *ideal self*, which is often contrasted with the *actual self*. Our *ideal self* is not only made up of qualities, such as warmth or unselfishness, but also particular goals, such as being a mother. But our *actual self*, the person we currently are, often falls short of this idealized persona. So, even subconsciously, we seek to use various means of getting closer to the *ideal self* that we want to become. The notion of the *ideal self* is different for every person. Some find themselves drawn to models of quiet servitude while others feel their strengths are best suited to lead others. But regardless of the pathway, one thing is clear. It almost never happens alone.

Those who are close to us can either aid or hamper our pathway to the *ideal self*. Research has identified a phenomenon called the *Michelangelo Phenomenon*, in which close partners, such as spouses, actually act as sculptors in illuminating and promoting a person's *ideal self*. They do this first by recognizing the difference between their significant other's *actual* versus *ideal self*, then finding supportive, yet directed ways to help their partner see these disparities, too. They affirm instances in which their partner is moving towards achieving their goals while finding daily ways, through regular behaviors, to make it easier for the *ideal self* to emerge. For example, if the significant other wants to become healthier, the partner not only praises steps made in this direction, but also finds ways to support this regularly, such as cooking better foods or watching the kids while he or she goes out for a run. Studies have indicated that when this occurs, not only does the significant other experience greater well-being, but the relationship also improves and is likely to last longer.

Something else happens, too. As noted by Dr. Roger Walsh in his seminal review, "Lifestyle and Mental Health", "So powerful is interpersonal rapport [regarding the Michelangelo Phenomenon] that couples can mold one another both psychologically and physically. They may even come to look more alike, as resonant emotions sculpt their facial muscles into similar patterns...[1]" (pg. 6) It appears that while striving to help the person attain his or her ideal self, a partner may end up having more impact than he or she would have ever known. In contrast, when a partner attempts to exert influence on their significant other in ways that are only consistent with the *partner's ideal self,* regardless of the significant other's own *ideal self,* the result is called the *Pygmalion Phenomenon.* This occurs when a partner believes that he or she "knows best" for their significant other, and attempts to force the significant other to conform in this way. Research has indicated that this typically results in poorer relationship satisfaction and personal well-being.

When it comes to the self, many people hold to the idea that each person is pretty much who he or she has always been. However, certain philosophers, such as Julian Baggini, challenge this notion. In his secular view of the self put forth in the book *Ego Trick,* he believes that we are ever-changing, and that our *self* is actually much more layered, and multi-faceted than we ever realize. He suggests that although we feel a certain lifelong continuity, the reality is that the *self* we know is always going through revision, often in response to our relationships. He asserts that who we are has a lot to do with the perceptions of our *self* that we and others hold dear.

For our kids, we must learn the difference between teaching values and knowledge versus directing them toward one particular calling. There is no question that we must seek to teach our kids right and wrong, and nurture in them a respect for values, such as faith and hard work, that many of us cherish. But along the way, we must be careful not overlay the criteria of our *ideal self* onto their own. This is especially true in adolescence, a time when identity issues emerge supreme. Years ago, I had a series of frank discussions with a father, who had been a long-time coach. He was struggling to come to grips with the person his son was becoming, partially because his son's goals seemed very different than his own. Although he recognized the positive, empathetic qualities his son conveyed, he mourned the loss of the *ideal vision* as he saw his son taking a different pathway than he would have chosen for his own.

It makes me wonder. If our ultimate purpose is to promote greater contentment and meaning in those closest to us, do our actions and behaviors coincide with this? Although it intuitively seems that the best way to get what we want from others is to "keep persisting until we wear them down," most of us, in moments of honest reflection, realize that a particular psychological principle remains true; that is, the more stubbornly we *pursue* others in search of *our* goals, the more they often *distance* themselves from us along the way. It serves as a reminder that each of us must seek to understand better what those closest to us see in their *ideal self,* and ask ourselves what *we are doing* to support this regardless of our own calling. When this happens, we may find out that they, in turn, will do the same for us. Good thing the moon and the sun will once again exchange admiring glances as another day recedes in anticipation of one starting anew...

† † † †

Supporting the ideal self of our significant other comes with a lot of fear. One of the challenges I have heard multiple times over the years in regards to this idea is "Well, what if I think that he or she is completely headed down the wrong road, or is losing his or her mind? Are you saying that I should simply support this because the other person feels this is the pathway they should take?"

There are a few points of clarification in order to really make this idea of "supporting the ideal self" clear. The first is the biblical mandate that all of us engage in fraternal correction. A little ways back I was very fortunate to hear a local priest, Fr. Tony Ernst, speak about this topic. He clearly addressed this topic, which had been broached in multiple readings that day. In the first reading, God had declared through Ezekiel (33:8) that, "If I tell the wicked, 'O wicked one, you shall surely die', and you do not speak out to dissuade the wicked from his way, the wicked shall die for his guilt, but I will hold you responsible for his death." As his sermon continued, Fr. Tony further delineated his own struggles to uphold this command. He spoke of his desire to avoid confrontation, to just keep his worries of others to himself, to allow faith to remain private. And yet, in the passion that rang through his own hesitancy, he proclaimed that we are to look out for each other in the pursuit of eternal salvation. "We are called to be watchmen" he said, even while suggesting that most of us would rather retreat in the night. True love, as spoken by Paul in the second reading, "is the fulfillment of the law." But in essence, I could hear Fr. Tony saying that true love is often tough love, the kind that his grandmother espoused (even when she was wrong) when she felt her family was going astray. We are called to watch over others in hopes that others will watch out for us.

Supporting a person's ideal self does not mean we abandon fraternal correction. In fact, it is necessary that we completely uphold it if we feel that something a person is doing, such as engaging in poor health practices or immoral activities, clearly undermines their ability to fully function as the human being God intended. Still, the manner in which we do this is so, so critical. If we come to the person with accusations and a sense that "we know best" and do not truly attempt to empathize through an understanding of what is occurring, then it is likely that the outcome of these conversations is going to lead to a greater distance between two people. But if we make observations, and express our concerns, there is a much better chance, although certainly not a guarantee, that we will be heard and further conversation will ensue. There is a big difference between saying to someone, "Why do you always smoke when people come over?" (in a derogatory way) then making the observation, "I notice that when friends come over you often go outside and smoke. I am concerned that this may be becoming a habit that might affect your health." Often the difficulty in providing feedback in the latter manner is that what we may feel we are asking, or demanding, is clearly reasonable and should be respected. Frankly, we might be right. But if our ultimate goal is to evoke long-term change, and not firstly to express our repeated frustration, then we are obliged to consider what action will most likely do this, even (or especially) if it takes "swallowing our pride."

The second issue that many struggle with around the concept of the *Michelangelo Phenomenon* is that they have difficulty letting go of control in marriage, and taking the leap of faith that this will actually result in greater consideration for each person's needs. Most people who grew up in the 50's or 60's would acknowledge that a patriarchal theme permeated many households in the United States. It was generally believed that when fathers got home from work, their toil should be done and that the wife was the one to take care of subsequent household tasks even if her day was as, or even more challenging, than that of the husband. As noted in an article published in the May 13th, 1955 edition of *Housekeeping Monthly*, a "good wife" should "make him comfortable", "arrange his pillow and offer to take off his shoes", "don't ask him questions about his actions or judgment or integrity..." among a multitude of other things that indicated that offsetting the stress of *his* day was far more important than offsetting the stress of *hers*[2]. Wives were often taught that husbands should be allowed to relax if desired for the rest of the evening even if it meant she was scurrying around until bedtime so that everything got done. We could reasonably argue that this was an incongruent situation—not because the husband and wife took on different roles, but simply because one persons' time and stress was considered more salient, and that expectations of effort, needs, and rest were not equally regarded.

Interestingly, a number of decades later, this may have actually shifted in the other direction, at least for certain areas. Take for example the "honey do list" that we so often hear wives giving their husbands. Ask yourself a few questions. Why is it that we (at least those I know and have discussed this subject with) never speak of the husbands giving their wives "honey do lists" or something of a similar kind? Recently, in fact, one of my coworkers joked that when (or if, especially after hearing his wife's comments) her husband went into retirement, she would be his "toughest boss ever." Now, many argue that these arrangements are functional, and even somewhat accepted, by many men. But I am not concerned about positions of functionality. I am most concerned about the values of a congruent, equal partnership explained in the prior discussion of basic rights which culminates in loving one another as yourself. I do not need another boss, another mother, even another caretaker. What I need is a wife, and what I hope that she needs most is a husband. Any arrangement that confuses this commitment into being something that it is not designed to be, whether it is "honey do lists" or anything else, threatens to undermine a true partnership in which each of us desires to support and promote the *ideal self* in the other.

When this occurs, it often threatens the health of the other person and our relationship as a whole. For example, if I demand that the house be perfectly clean, dinner to always be ready, and all household chores to be completed, just when and how am I supporting the physical health of my wife? As importantly, what happens when one spouse feels repeatedly "told" what to do in a way that does not promote constant sharing. Gregory Popcak argues in his book, *The Exceptional Seven Percent,* that in the best marital relationships, spouses are never told they absolutely must or cannot do certain things. His contention is that the best marriages involve a constant, dynamic discussion of each person's needs, desires, and callings. His sense, based on a large body of research, is that the spouses in these marriages work to support each person's ideal self through transparent communication that involves observation, reflection, and constructive brainstorming. In the process, spouses come to have greater influence on the other person than those relationships in which more controlling, even degrading methods, are used. Exceptional couples come to realize that the fear which may come in supporting their partner's ideal self is much less based in reality than the fear that comes with the realization that a partner has distanced themselves from them. When this occurs, and the likelihood of influence decreases, it is here that serious threats to each person, and the relationship as a whole, become realized.

Yet in truly understanding what it means to support another's *ideal self*, it is worth going back to those earliest days of wooing and attraction. Very often, as the years of a relationship increase, people become embroiled in the responsibilities and roles that each person has, and forget what truly brought both individuals together in the first place. So consider this. What aspects of your partner's beauty first led you to consider him or her as potentially more than a friend? Was it her caring, compassionate demeanor? Artistic skills? Humorous personality? Physical health and beauty? Psychological curiosity? Commitment to those least fortunate?

Now, ask yourself this. Just how much are you doing now to support these qualities in him or her? I certainly don't want to imply that just because someone was an athlete in high school that this automatically means that their *ideal self* twenty years later includes this same goal. But, the reality is that for most of us, many of the interests or pursuits that we developed in our early years still remain of interest and importance now, even if buried under layers and layers of adult responsibilities and demands. What if, though, your husband committed himself to finding ways to still make their pursuit possible, as an inlet or even just as side pursuit? How much would this mean to you, and potentially your marriage, if he did this?

Consider this from a few different angles. Not only would this would potentially better fulfill the promise of the *Michelangelo Phenomenon*, but it also seems that it could go a long way towards preserving those entities that were so critical towards first uniting the couple in a romantic pursuit. This again does not imply that couple can't, and shouldn't evolve, in the ways that they maintain love for each other. For example, I find myself so often moved (and attracted to) my wife when I watch and listen to her read for our children, as it is just one beautiful illustration of how she is so committed to their development, and in love with them. This was something I never would have considered before we had kids. But I would be dishonest in saying that I am not attracted to her physical beauty and athletic, healthful pursuits, ever since I came to know her as a volleyball player in high school. I know she would say the same about me. So although we both don't play volleyball or football any longer, we go to great efforts to support each other's athletic endeavors, which these days come through regular endurance and triathlon training. Although this requires a significant amount of coordination and effort, it remains a big piece of our relationship, and therefore, leads us to prioritize this over other potential tasks, such as frequently washing the car or keeping the house in pristine condition.

Each couple has their own areas of attraction and unity that are important, and many would not cite athletic or even health endeavors as part of this list. However, I have come to believe for many reasons, including that of my work as a psychologist, that couples who pursue physical and psychological health together, just as those that pursue prayer together, are more likely to find a basis that provides for constant renewal, flexibility, and commitment. Just as regular, unitive prayer is so important for our pursuit of eternal salvation and spiritual endeavors on earth, and to work through daily challenges, so unitive health practices seem critical to both our daily needs and ability to engage each other in a clarified, cleansed way.

What happens with many couples when they do not share a health consciousness is that they often struggle to find both individual and collective ways to deal with stress appropriately and seem more inclined to seek out methods of tension reduction that may be both unhealthy and/or disconnected from each other. This does not necessarily mean that partners have to engage in these practices together (although this also can provide opportunities to connect and unify), but simply having a constant focus on providing opportunities for the other to remain healthy sends a very clear message. That message is as follows: "Your health and well-being is of utmost importance to me, more than any other responsibility that you have." Of course, as with anything, such foci can be taken to extremes, but it is not generally the case.

But what about the responsibility of raising kids, you might say? Well, again, we start with two simple premises. One, you can only give what you have, especially to your children that need you most. Mothers especially who do not provide for themselves in the four primary areas of dimension are not only at significant risk themselves for many issues, but put their kids at increased risk, too. This is never better illustrated than by the extensive research on maternal depression. Maternal depression, especially for those that have young kids, is one of the biggest risk factors for negative outcomes for children in almost any imaginable area, whether it be academic, psychological, social, physical, or otherwise. It truly goes without saying that the best thing mothers can do for their youth is take care of themselves first. Remember, when the plane starts going down, you are always told to put your oxygen mask on first before doing so for your child.

The second reason that this is critical is that when spouses look out for each other's health and well-being, it is one more way of sending the clear message that the most important date in a married household is not the day the children were born, but the anniversary date. Repeatedly we see that when alliances start to form between a parent and a child that supersede the authority and bond of two parents, negative outcomes are likely to occur. Children naturally seek out parents who are more accommodating for their needs and desires. Although this partly can result in a positive, nurturing situation, when this occurs repeatedly as a way of undermining the stricter parent, it sets up one more dynamic in which a parental and/or spousal role becomes skewed in an unhealthy way.

As a final consideration of the *ideal self*, and for that matter, the *ideal marriage*, we understand that no one ever fully attains this designation just as no one ever reaches the pinnacle of divine perfection we are called to pursue. But in giving of ourselves to our significant other so that a harmonic wholeness may emerge, we may find a similar course of our own. When spouses work to shed the layers of triviality and superficiality, and meet each other whether they are, and where they are called to be, a new collective dimension emerges that was likely not seen before. Although their actions and goals may still be different at times, it is as if a collective unconscious begins to operate, one in which a set of universal principles increasingly guides what they pursue. It seems here that we may come to really experience what it means to be made in the image and likeness of God, both in the sacrament of baptism and in the sacrament of holy matrimony. We acknowledge our faults and fallacies. But the vision of my oneness, with Him and her, becomes a radiant, guiding light that is impossible to ignore.

The Psychological Dimension

Do not be conformed to this world, but be transformed by the renewal of your mind, that by testing you may discern what is the will of God, what is good and acceptable and perfect.

Romans 12:2

15

Where Mental *Health* Begins

The greatest discovery of my generation is that human beings can alter their lives by altering their attitudes of mind.
—William James

In 1980, my father started the Can Collector's Club (CCC). I was 2 years old. As the story goes, it was my mother's brainchild, but dad quickly took ahold of the idea with his entrepreneurial spirit. Some people thought he had lost his mind. Some still do. But the purpose of the CCC was simple. Convince family and friends to turn aluminum cans into him so that he could use the money from recycling to support our college fund. And clean up the environment. Quickly, the CCC turned into an annual contest, with those collecting the most cans awarded prizes at a fiscal (can) year-end party that featured balloon tosses, a self-indulgent speech by the director himself (often in costume), and a cast of characters set on taking irreverence to a whole new level. As the years passed with semi-annual newsletters, and the number of cans grew, so did the stories, enough so that one day, Jim Schroeder (Sr.), ended up on the front page of CNN.com. Midst the eccentricities and obsessiveness at times, though, my father remained ever *conscious* of his goals. Even his arguments grew more *coherent* as the dollars amassed and the number of families involved grew. And ever *conscientious* of his children's needs and the community of people that rallied around this cause, he began to look at other ways to have a positive effect on those who needed it most.

So it is when it comes to mental health. As the Diagnostic of Statistical Manual of Mental Disorders (DSM-5) tops out at a whopping 947 pages, and the National Institutes of Mental Health (NIMH) promises millions of dollars in search of biological causes for mental conditions, something seems lost in trying to really understand where mental *health* really begins. Mental *health* is not the absence of impairing, abnormal, or distressing symptoms any more than summer is the absence of ice, snow, and cold. Summer is a period of great growth just as we humans are beings of tremendous possibility. But in order to be mentally healthy, three things must be present: *consciousness, coherence,* and *conscientiousness.* By nature, these mind states are active processes and apply to both our internal experiences and our external behaviors.

Consciousness is not just a dynamic awareness of our thoughts and feelings, but it is an acute understanding and concern of our circumstances, now and at other times. Put more simply, it is a person's ability to take in their situation fully in order to best determine their next course of action. *Coherence* is the state of being logical, consistent, and congruent with what exists around us. It does not disregard our emotional state, but it mandates that the arguments we make be based on reasonable facts, ideas, and/or beliefs. *Conscientiousness* signifies that what we do is right and just, and that our actions are principled. It serves as our link to others, in that we consider how they are affected by our behaviors.

For arguments sake, take any diagnosed mental condition, and you will find that each of these three critical factors are at play. When we are depressed, we become less conscious to the world around us, our beliefs become irrational, and self-absorption takes hold. When we cannot concentrate, we tend to only focus on loosely connected details, our thoughts become disjointed and confusing, and we seek to satisfy the need that lies right in front of us.

But this is not about pathology. It is about health. It is why exercise works so well to improve mental health. When you are physically fit, your mind becomes more *conscious* to what is going on. With this, comes an opportunity to step outside your closed box and consider what you and others may see and need. It is why cognitive-behavioral therapy works. It seeks to take irrational beliefs and put them into a clearer, more realistic context. The belief that "Everyone hates me" is no more *coherent* than the grandiose idea that "Everyone loves me." It is why regular volunteering has long been known to have lasting positive psychological effects on the volunteer. We become *conscientious* of the fact that we are not the only one with a tough life.

So before we get so entangled in mental dysfunction, maybe we need to spend some more time considering what happens when we really do function. In the process, we may find that stigma reduces, conversations become more productive, and we all begin to realize that your mind and my mind need to focus on developing the same critical properties. And if anything or anyone tries to convince you that a mobile device or a pill can take the place of these things, be very, very cautious. Nothing can take their place, and sometimes, that which promises to relieve you can leave you more scattered and disjointed than before.

By the way, for those who are curious, the CCC is in its 36th year running. This past year, a record number of families (60) participated. Now that all of my siblings have graduated college, 100% of the proceeds (including that from my father's penny and nickel clubs) go to a mission in Haiti, where my father can't wait to go every year to see the beautiful, shining faces of those kids he loves. His vision, and that of my mother's, remains just as *conscious*, *coherent*, and *conscientious* as ever. And now, a new generation has gotten into the mix, as my kids and their cousins scramble over wooded banks and scour sidewalks for cans amid the questioning gazes of onlookers, who can only wonder just what possesses those kids to do such a thing.

† † † †

When we speak of mental health, or psychological well-being, we find ourselves in a confluence of opinion. Over the past few decades, much has occurred in the treatment of mental illness, or distressing circumstances of any description or kind. One of the trends is to further define categories to a minute degree for the supposed purpose of allowing for better communication, classification, and research. The original DSM published in 1952 was 130 pages. As noted earlier, the 5th edition of DSM is almost a 1,000 pages. We now have names for almost every imaginable symptom and condition. Unlike previous DSM editions, DSM-5 also no longer includes any formal axis symptom to list medical and psychosocial issues that might be contributing to an individual's condition(s). Regardless of what has been said, this makes it appear that conditions diagnosed are inherent to the psychological state of the assessed individual, not necessarily a result of environmental, familial, and/or many other factors.

Meanwhile, certain governing bodies, including NIMH, find themselves taking a different course as they continue to seek out clear biological causes of mental conditions. The findings to this point have been underwhelming, and although it was once thought that deficiencies or an excess of neurotransmitters (e.g., serotonin) were once directly responsible for afflictions such as depression, it is clear now that the brain's complexity was sorely underestimated. But the search goes on for these biological and/or genetic causes.

What remains is a gaping hole. As individuals and governing bodies continue their search for refining categories and organic causes, there is a risk that once again, we will attempt to divorce our psychological health from that of our other dimensions. The positive news is that increased research has illuminated physical and social correlates to poor mental health, and has also gone in search of understanding just how individuals remain resilient in the face of significant odds.

Yet the disconnection between where the research is headed, and our practical attempts to actually look at how our mental health is being afflicted by poor health in other areas, remains significant. In 2013, Abilify, an atypical antipsychotic drug, was the number one medication in total sales not just in regards to psychiatric drugs, but all legal drugs[1]. Psychiatric drugs in general have flooded the market, and are prescribed most heavily by primary care physicians. The number of mental health professionals also has grown, and although valid arguments can be made that therapy remains underutilized, access to this service remains at an all-time high. Some do benefit from treatments. But many, many people continue to languish, and statistics regarding mental health difficulties only seem to be getting direr. In 2011, 41.4 million adults in the US reported having a mental illness in the past year[2]. It is a strange, and humbling situation, especially for someone like me who is supposed to be part of a solution.

Once again, it appears that the solution may lie outside the prototypical mental health field. Convincing evidence suggests that negative trends in sleep, media/technology use, nutrition, physical activity, and faith all are likely associated with increased rates of psychological distress and mental conditions. Research has long shown that faith, spirituality, and religion as a whole are buffering, coping strategies for mental health issues, especially when an individual has a close relationship with a higher power. Intuitively, many of us know this, but would it be true to say that when it comes to our psychological health, there is no substitute for God? This is what A.J Cronin clearly thought when he said:

> Above all am I convinced of the need, irrevocable and inescapable, of every human heart, for God. No matter how we try to escape, to lose ourselves in restless seeking, we cannot separate ourselves from our divine source. There is no substitute for God.

If it is true that in our attempt to substitute many other interventions, or vices, for God, we find ourselves less psychological healthy, this still deserves further clarification. It is not enough to point out statistics which indicate that we are going to church less than we did just a few decades ago. It seems lacking to simply blame the increased secularization of our public square. Even the proliferation of materialization likely falls short of an explanation. Valid contentions can be made that each of these are playing a role in our psychological demise. Yet each seems to fall short of full explanation.

But as Cronin noted, we must begin with the "need...of every human heart, for God." We must begin with that relationship, and those that foster that relationship from an early age. If faith and mental health are inextricably linked, then it appears that relationships which foster and nurture faith, religion, and a relationship with God from an early age, are themselves linked closely, too.

In the search, though, we find that our desires, and feelings, will wax and wane. It is here that faith practices must be learned, and covenants be kept even when we feel forsaken that God, or Love, is not to be found. If psychology and faith are as closely aligned as we are starting to see, then the reuniting of these old friends begins with the understanding that practices which underlie the former have always been necessary for the latter. Whether it is happiness or holiness that we seek, we may find that lanes seemingly once diverged suddenly merge into solitary, wooded trail winding up a hill.

16

Turning Distress into Joy

Forgiveness is not always easy. At times, it feels more painful than the wound we suffered, to forgive the one that inflicted it. And yet, there is no peace without forgiveness
—Marianne Williamson

Part I: Forgiveness

On the night of January 21, 1995, Azim Khamisa's life changed forever. While delivering pizza, his 20-year-old son, Tariq Khamisa, was shot and killed by Tony Hicks, a 14-year-old gang member. Set to be married to his girlfriend, Tariq would never see his wedding day. Neither would his father. Days and months went by, and Azim struggled to get out of bed, to even take the simplest steps towards the next day. But as life dragged on, Azim began to sense that something extraordinary would have to occur in order for him to survive, and thrive again. He would have to forgive his son's killer.

As described in a CBS interview[1], Azim felt he needed to take some responsibility for the tragic death of his own son. He started by forgiving Tony Hick's family, and eventually forged a friendship with his guardian and grandfather, Ples Felix. He then founded the Tariq Khamisa Foundation (TKF) in honor of his son, with the purpose of reducing youth violence by reaching students at various ages. Founded on six key tenets, the Foundation, which provides services and mentorship to over 20,000 students annually, begins with the idea that "Violence is real and hurts us all" and ends with the belief

"From conflict, love and unity are possible." But Azim's story did not end there. Five years after his son's life was ended by an arbitrary bullet, Azim stared into eyes of his murderer. He saw himself. Then, he forgave Tony, and offered him a job at his Foundation if and when he would be released from prison. Tony is up for parole in 2027.

All of us hope that we never are asked to face the reality that Azim was forced to confront. Most of us struggle to understand how we could find the resolve to forgive someone in the way that he did. But none of us have the luxury of not being hurt by others, in the infinite number of ways this can occur. Over the past 20 years, the time-honored virtue of forgiveness has been subjected to a huge scientific inquiry. A simple PsycINFO search of "forgiveness" uncovers almost 3,000 citations regarding a deeper review into what has become accepted as an effective therapeutic technique for traumatic experiences, whether it be chronic child abuse, random acts of violence, or institutional warfare. Forgiveness has consistently been shown to be associated with better psychological and physical health[2]. Large scales have shown that forgiving others is associated with less anxiety, depressive symptoms, and perceived stress[3].

But the models of forgiveness differ, and the misconceptions abound although some like Mr. Khamisa, take particularly exceptional steps to move forward. As C.S. Lewis once said,

> ...forgiving does not mean excusing. Many people seem to think it does. They think that if you ask them to forgive someone who has cheated or bullied them you are trying to make out that there was really no cheating or no bullying. But if that

were so, there would be nothing to forgive. They keep on replying, "But I tell you the man broke a most solemn promise." Exactly: that is precisely what you have to forgive. (This doesn't mean that you must necessarily believe his next promise. It does mean that you must make every effort to kill every taste of resentment in your own heart— every wish to humiliate or hurt him or to pay him out.)

Interestingly, too, forgiveness is often more of an intrapersonal process, than an interpersonal one. In a study looking at small sample of individuals from Western Australia exposed to severe trauma, one theme kept coming through as with other research. Participants reported that forgiveness had much more to do with themselves than the offender. In reconciling what had occurred, and in releasing much of the guilt and pain and anger that they held so close, there was a sense of "letting go" that allowed for the possibility that tomorrow just might be different, and even better, than today[4]. But in order for this to happen, it seemed there must be an awareness of just how the circumstances, and their subsequent reaction, had changed the course of their lives. In doing so, many experienced a new perspective of the offender (not necessarily to be confused with unconditional positive regard), one less jaded with attributions of absolute evil, but more colored with the imperfections that existed within all humanity, including themselves.

But for some, like Mr. Khamisa, this process leads to what is termed "interpersonal reconciliation sentiment" (IPS) and unconditional forgiveness. IPS is defined as

"...the personal, intimate feeling of being reconciled, at least to a certain level, with the people who have severely harmed you" expressed into "the resumption of some amount of trust and collaboration." Research into those affected in the 1994 Rwandan genocide found that most of the perpetrators of violence did not apologize, and yet people were left to find a way to move forward in the midst of the disharmony that abounded[5]. Findings indicated it was not only necessary for personal growth, but also critical for societal well-being, and rebuilding, as a whole. As Nelson Mandela stated on his inauguration day, after 27 years in prison, "The time for the healing of the wounds has come. The moment to bridge the chasms that divide us has come. The time to build is upon us."

Regardless of the path taken, though, it appears that the necessity of forgiveness is born of a few different dimensions. One is what I will call personal and political effectiveness. It is clear that while rage and distrust can spawn awareness and discussions of misdoings and maltreatment, it cannot sustain a unitive, long-standing movement towards a larger goal of recognizing just how seven billion, imperfect human beings could co-exist in an authentic, yet peaceful way. Those who never find ways to reconcile with imperfect manifestation of others, and instead focus on the failures that may arise, will struggle mightily to move beyond their own constituency of bitterness. Reiterating Lewis, forgiveness does not mean excusing or forgetting, especially as we go in search of a better way. But it does mean acknowledging—of which we are flawed, of which we are failed, of which we are all in need of mercy.

Forgiveness also breeds from a deeper understanding, which is that our life may not be what we expected, or even desired. As Mr. Khamisa must have felt he was posed the very unfair question, "Do I choose my pride, or do I chose my life, just not as I would have had it?" It seems very doubtful that even in the midst of his forgiveness, he still does not experience periodic spikes of anger, and of loss—for he did lose his son. But as with every great heroic act, forgiveness requires daily, willful acts and reminders that I am opening myself to a different pathway, which is especially difficult when the reminders of transgressions remain palpable, such as ongoing physical issues that stem from an offense. For many, this is partly why forgiveness and faith are intertwined so tightly, as there is an acceptance that my life is not my own while I strive to live in communion with others. But my life is one that I choose to open myself to each day, and not allow the walls within to close ever more tightly when suffering presents itself. Ironically, although the intrapersonal model suggests forgiveness is self-serving, others left in our "distraught wake" may suggest that in serving ourselves, we are serving others in a much better way.

The human condition is both incredibly unique and yet so much the same. Our experiences are as vast as the oceans and as similar as the atoms that comprise them. Our calls range from the most secluded of hermits to the most exposed of world leaders. But we are all faced with betrayal and disappointment. We are all faced with each other. And if we choose to take on what life has given us, and open ourselves to others, then it sure seems we have an implicit understanding that we must forgive. A few years ago, I attended a wedding in which the groom and his only brother were estranged over what seemed to be a minor issue. His brother did not show for the ceremony.

Although I knew little of the details, I was greatly saddened that two raised so closely could move so far away, and forego one of, if not the, most important day of their lives. It seems that a long road of forgiveness must ensue if the bonds of their brotherhood will resume, and they live to teach their children how to love again. So it seems for us, too.

A fine line separates our angels from our demons.
   —Shane Neimeyer

Part II: Channeling

  Shane Neimeyer had just tried to hang himself. It, too, had failed. Like much of his life to that point, which had been spent in and out of state custody since his adolescent years, his road had hit a dead end. But in the depths of his despair, thoughts of a different kind surfaced, with one idea in mind: Ironman. Sitting in his straight jacket, awaiting sentencing as a homeless heroin addict, he had turned the pages of an endurance magazine to pass the time. As he began to read more about triathlons, there was something about the discipline, the drive, the pursuit of a difficult goal, which began to consume him. The thought entered his mind. Maybe he could be one of them. Maybe his life could change forever.

  His troubles began as a teen in Central Illinois[6]. By the time he was 18, he had already been arrested for theft, burglary, and driving under the influence. After skipping out on college at Colorado State University, his drug addiction only worsened as he found himself on the streets of Boise, Idaho. By the time all of his sentencing was over, he would land in jail 25 times. He began exercising intensively during his stays, often running laps around the small courtyard. In 2005, he placed 50th overall in his first half Ironman held in Bend, Oregon with a time of 5 hours, 8 minutes. In 2010, he landed himself in the granddaddy of all triathlons, the World Championships in Kona. It was the year he finally said goodbye to official state supervision of any kind.

Today, Shane is a strength and conditioning coach in Boulder, Colorado. He has now done eight full Ironman triathlons, and continues to train intensively. In talking about his life, he often discusses how the "neurotic, excessive personality traits" that fueled drug addiction and a life of high-risk crime are the same kind that enabled him, like others, to become an elite athlete. Although he acknowledges that he still thinks about his former life, he credits his dramatic change to triathlons. As he said, "Triathlons gave me what I desperately needed: a purpose."

Beneath each purpose that propels our lives, we are driven by a daily source of energy that is difficult to define, but impossible to ignore. Bred of genetic underpinnings, individual experiences, immediate surroundings, collective culture, and other influences, this unique energy begins to manifest itself early in our lives. Expressed as desires, urges, compulsions, curiosities, drives, interests, or any other given name, this energy gradually becomes known as part of our personality. In actuality, it is a dynamic, daily interplay of what I simply will call drives (for ease of communication) that is an ever-evolving, unique sense of self that interfaces with the world we live. Often, our varied drives are easily satisfied in ways that are considered acceptable by us and others. Sometimes they are not. When a particular drive reveals itself within us that can result in negative consequences, like in Shane's situation, we find ourselves a serious quandary. Although directions from caregivers or peers may be to simply squelch the desire, this may not work. If we can squelch negative energy, we are left with two primary options, although these are not always consciously chosen. The first is to continue with similar behaviors as before, and accept the possible consequences as Shane did with his drug use and criminal activity. The second is to find a more acceptable outlet for the particular energies that exist. This is where channeling becomes crucial.

Channeling as used here is defined "a way, course, or direction of thought or action" as in "new *channels* of exploration". It is the process by which we define novel pathways and new outlets for a specific drive or state that may otherwise be undesirable. Although channeling could technically occur in a negative way, the focus here is on using energy in a positive, productive manner.

In some ways, we do this every day probably without even realizing it. If we are feeling stressed after work, we may channel this into a run. If we are worried about an upcoming event and can't sleep, we may get out of bed and clean. We might use a journal entry to create a narrative to channel our sadness. We might mow the yard to harness the "edge" we feel after a long day at work. But, for more chronic states of drive that can cause us or others harm or disruption, it is critically important to figure out a way to transform this energy in a way that will do good, or at least, not wrong. In some ways, channeling is closely related, but not synonymous with sublimation. Although sublimation is often associated with a psychoanalytic perspective, the broader meaning of the term is "to divert the expression of (an instinctual desire or impulse) from its unacceptable form to one that is considered more socially or culturally acceptable." It applies to any drive that may consume or divert us to behaviors that contradict our particular values or calls. In Shane's case, he literally created a new pathway, a new life from the same drives and compulsions that almost destroyed him. The drive never left, but the way in which he satisfied the drive changed dramatically.

One way in which this can be important for some is in regards to hostility and aggressive behavior. Hostility has long been shown to be associated with negative health outcomes, including heart disease[7]. Some research has indicated that we can channel aggressive or hostile impulses[8]. But, it appears that our ability to do this is affected by our conscious beliefs about how aggressive we perceive ourselves to be, and our implicit acceptance of rationales for a particular aggressive act. In other words, if we believe we are an aggressive, hostile person, and rationalize why another person or entity deserves our hostility or violent behavior, we are less likely to channel these behaviors to more acceptable, and at times, useful alternatives. Therefore, in order to channel aggression, we must first address the beliefs and assumptions that we hold about ourselves and others. As with forgiveness, channeling does not mean that we forego a courageous, and at times, militant pathway toward undoing wrongs being done. But it does mean we attempt to harness this energy in a way that is productive, not destructive, in a manner we do not intend.

This seems very much what John Walsh did after the brutal murder of his six-year-old son, Adam. He went from building luxury hotels to a lifetime of anti-crime activism. Although not without his own controversy, it appears that he channeled his rage towards a murderer never convicted (the alleged killer died in prison on a life sentence for other crimes before going to trial) in trying to help others avoid a similar fate. His ability to channel his anger productively was a key in aiding justice for many people.

Another form of channeling is also used to treat tics in children and adults in the empirically-supported method of habit reversal training (HRT). Once a person recognizes a premonitory urge that immediately precedes the tic, they are taught how to channel this involuntary urge into a voluntary behavior that closely resembles the original tic, but draws less attention from others. For example, a tic that involves shaking the head side-to-side repeatedly may be replaced with tensing the neck in place, and pushing the chin towards the chest while deep breathing. Gradually, these behaviors are often shaped into other actions that become manageable and less frequent.

Over the past few decades, studies have increasingly shown just how predictive self-control in youth is when it comes to almost any important outcome as adults[9]. Studies have also shown that self-control, unlike intelligence and other factors, is very malleable and sustaining. With our own kids, my wife and I try to teach awareness and self-discipline daily. But as I watch them grow, and I see the various drives and urges spring forth, I am become increasingly convinced that the formation of self-control and self-channeling are, and must be, intertwined. Whereas one may sit through a church service without much challenge, another one really struggles to inhibit the instinctive urges that come with an hour in the pews. Simply rehashing the same old redirections about willpower or consequences may not be enough, for them or for us. We must get creative and persistent, in teaching a skill, however challenging it is now, that could spawn a lifetime of promise. No matter the age or circumstance, like Shane, it is never too late to channel our drives in a manner that not only benefits us, but also others as well. In doing so, we may do much more than avoid potential negative outcomes. We may begin to thrive in ways we would have never dreamed even if life gets really trying.

No one is useless in this world who lightens the burdens of others.   —Charles Dickens

Part III: Helping Others

As noted prior, research on volunteering has long found that those who help others have better physical health and psychological adjustment. And it's not just that healthy individuals seek out ways to help others more; it is that in helping others that we reap the benefits of better well-being, too. Not only do we feel better but, for youth especially, there is a decrease in risk-taking behaviors, and more prosocial actions, especially with those outside of their family. But why is this the case?

One, it appears that volunteering and helping behaviors enhance eudaimonic [yoo-dey-mon-ik] well-being, which should be distinguished from hedonic well-being. Hedonic well-being suggests that happiness and contentment comes from seeking out pleasurable activities (and avoiding pain), such as eating something sweet or winning a prize. In contrast, eudaimonic well-being is rooted in the belief that happiness comes from participating in activities that involve a deeper purpose or meaning. Hedonic activities can lead us to feel good, but only eudaimonic activities, such as volunteering, can lead us to feel good *about ourselves*. This is the essence of eudaimonic well-being. Actions focused on helping others or our world help us feel that we matter.

The concept of *mattering* was introduced in 1981 by Morris Rosenberg and Claire McCullough[10]. They defined it as the perception that we are a significant part of the world around us—that people notice us, care that we exist, and value who we are. Multiple studies indicate that mattering plays a key role in why helping others leads to better well-being. When we feel valued and needed by other people, we feel better about ourselves.

Findings also indicate that those who are least socially integrated end up benefitting the most from helping others[11]. It appears that those who are isolated, have few close relationships, and struggle to be part of a social network are the very ones whose lives can be changed dramatically by giving their time for charitable causes. This is especially important for victims of abuse and maltreatment as many are left feeling disconnected and estranged from those around them. In striving to regain a sense of interpersonal unity through layers of intense anxiety and insecurity, being a helper (in whatever capacity it may be) provides a universal opportunity for victims to bridge their vulnerability with that of others. As Holly discovered in the story below, this moment of connection can spawn a new light of hope, a resurrected glimpse into a humanness that may have been long lost.

The process of helping others also brings stark reminders of just how resilient we can be. In their own bitter pain, helpers can come to know others whose stories seem as bad, or even worse, than their own. And yet repeatedly, through tales of faith or persistence or survival, they are faced with victims that look less like victims, and more like warriors and transcenders. An introspective process can ensue, challenging whether the helper's victim status is quite as impenetrable as was previously believed. Thoughts of resurgence seep in as an encounter with others in struggle challenges the helper to rewrite his or her tragic story into a revival. A new will emerges. A new love filters in.

Holly's Story

She could hear a train rumbling through. Lying on her stomach, all she could think about was staying alive. Minutes earlier, she watched in horror as her boyfriend, Chris, was bludgeoned to death with a large rock. She talked and pleaded with her captor, in hopes that her life would be spared.

The night had started out like any other in the town of Lexington, Kentucky. Holly and Chris had left a party nearby to take walk on the tracks[12]. Little did they know that Angel Resendiz, later to be known as the "Railroad Killer," had been watching them as they strolled

181

along. Suddenly, he appeared with a sharp weapon in hand. He tied and gagged them, forcing them to the side of the tracks. He seemed uninterested in money or other items they offered.

After being raped, the last thing she remembered was being hit repeatedly across the face with a wooden board. She lost consciousness, and woke up in someone's front yard. She would become the only known survivor of Resendiz's horrific killing spree.

After being treated at the hospital, she attempted to quickly return to her college life. Few knew what had happened since her name was not reported due to fears her assailant would try to locate her. By one year later, though, panic attacks increased and her grades were slipping. Anxiety gripped her at any moment.

Although anxiety remained, she gradually took steps in reclaiming her life. Along the way, she found that her deepest healing occurred in helping others traumatized by sexual abuse. Armed with her own traumatic experience and a no-nonsense demeanor, she instantly connected with children and parents in the throes of deep distress. She opened the nonprofit Holly's House in her hometown of Evansville, Indiana, where victims of abuse could be interviewed in a safe, comfortable setting.

No one desires tragedies and despair. But what if in our sorrow, we are given a unique chance to reach others seemingly unreachable, even if that be ourselves? In our lifetime, we may not always have a choice about to whom we matter. Those of whom we desire may reject us.

Schroeder

Those of whom we tire may accept us. But we can always matter to someone.

Gratitude is the healthiest of all human emotions. The more you express gratitude for what you have, the more likely you will have even more to express gratitude for.

—Zig Ziglar

Part IV: Gratitude

Tears were streaming down his mother's face. Just minutes earlier, he had unleashed a flurry of harsh statements and cursed at her as she stood their silently. For months, John Foppe's parents had tried to provide various options, and even personal encounters with others similar to him, to teach him how to do the basics. Like dressing himself. Or eating without assistance. Or using the restroom on his own. But over and over, John had refused to open himself to these possibilities, and was resigned to a life largely dependent on others. His parents struggled with what to do next. But, the night before, they had spoken with his brothers, and told them that they were no longer to help him unless told otherwise. They had decided it was time that John started learning how to do these things on his own. In a moment John later described as one of the most important in his life, his mother walked out of the room to leave him to put his clothes on. He failed. But, lying naked on the floor all alone, he suddenly "accepted that the miracle I had so desperately wanted wasn't going to happen...I also came to the point at which I realized that my anger at God had brought me no relief, only further pain" (p. 46).

John Foppe had been born with no arms, among a number of other serious congenital abnormalities. Doctors questioned whether he would survive at all. In his deeply motivating book, *What's Your Excuse? Making the Most Out of What You Have*. John describes his life of growing up with no arms into one of full independence, and his feelings of stigmatization and isolation even in the midst of support from others. In the depths of his struggle, John also notes evident gratitude in what most perceived as a very unfair situation. He expresses his appreciation for moments of tough love, and for many people that were willing to help. He speaks with graciousness for opportunities to take on new challenges, to experience natural surroundings, to know others more deeply. But most of all, he illustrates how growing up with no arms offered him an unusual chance to discover a unique perspective, a unique calling that ultimately helped him overcome many fears and obstacles, not just the ones presented by his missing appendages. What may sound really strange to some people is that John Foppe became thankful that he had no arms, even though much of life would have been easier with them.

Before we can really discuss what authentic gratitude is, though, it seems we address what gratitude is not. Gratitude is not false positivity or the denial of negative emotions. Gratitude is not condoning atrocities and maltreatment by others, even if an outcome might be good. As was noted by Christina Enevoldsen in her blog, false gratitude can lead to negative outcomes that span generations[13]. Being thankful also does not mean being tragically idealistic, or blind to obvious realities. True gratitude does not encourage settling, or an erosion of high standards, even if struggles highlight meaningful moments and progress that may remain hidden to untrained eyes.

The word gratitude itself is derived from both the Latin word *gratus*, meaning pleasing, and *grātitūdin-* (stem of *grātitūdō*), indicating thankfulness. It speaks to not only an act of graciousness, but also positive feelings originating from this deed. Studies have noted that it is endorsed as a universal character strength across countless cultures and creeds[14]. Research has also indicated that gratitude can have a number of significant, long-lasting positive effects on an individual[15,16]. In addition to physiological improvements, such as decreased blood pressure and improved immune function, gratitude has been consistently shown to improve social-emotional outcomes in the area of anxiety, depression, and substance use. As a specific therapeutic technique, gratitude can be effective for multiple issues.

In one particular study, a gratitude intervention was compared to four other positive-based strategies to determine whether each would increase levels of happiness and reduce depressive symptoms[17]. Participants were simply asked to write and deliver a letter to someone that they had never properly thanked. Results indicated that in comparison to other experimental strategies (e.g., focused on using/identifying strengths, recognizing good things in life), the "gratitude visit" group showed far and away the biggest increase in happiness and decrease in depressive symptoms on the immediate post-test. Evidence suggests, however, that repeated acts of gratitude are most likely to be associated with long-term benefits. As noted previously, it appears that the direct experience of gratitude, even fleeting, is incompatible with misery and distress. In giving thanks, we recognize a gain, no matter how small; at least for a moment, we let go of our sense of loss.

For those who have experienced significant trauma, gratitude interventions are gaining increasing recognition as effective means for progress. Studies have consistently found that Post Traumatic Stress Disorder (PTSD) levels are negatively correlated with post-trauma gratitude, independent of trauma severity, chronicity, and time elapsed since the traumatic event[18,19]. In other words, increased thankfulness was connected with decreased anxiety, flashback, and hypervigilance regardless of the characteristics of what happened. Gratitude not only provides *intra*personal benefits for the gracious person. It also provides *inter*personal connections for those who have been traumatized to maintain and expand their network of support. As unfortunately often happens, people suffering with significant psychological distress can "wear down" others through repeated solicitation of assistance and comfort. Acts of gratitude provide a unique opportunity to repair these strained bonds.

In really understanding the essence of gratitude, it is important to recognize that gratitude extends much beyond a pleasing act of graciousness. As eloquently described in the article, "Gratitude as a Psychotherapeutic Intervention" written by Robert Emmons and Robin Stern, gratitude is composed of two key components[20]. One, there is an assertion of "goodness" that exists in a person's life. But beyond this, there is a clear understanding that at least some of this goodness lies outside the individual. For many, gratitude is not just a worldly transaction, but elemental of a transcendent link. It exemplifies a sense that we are all part of a mysterious, interconnected, interdependent network. As Emmons and Stern noted:

> True gratefulness rejoices in the other. Its ultimate goal is to reflect back the goodness that one has received by creatively seeking opportunities for giving. The motivation for doing so resides in the grateful appreciation that one has lived by the grace of others. In this sense, the spirituality of gratitude is opposed to a self-serving belief that one deserves or is entitled to the blessings that he or she enjoys. (p. 847)

Some may question whether gratitude can be taught as a lifetime practice, or simply that it is acquired intrinsically or experientially in different ways. KIPP, the Knowledge is Power Program, is a national network of free, open-enrollment, college-preparatory public charter schools with a track record of preparing students in underserved communities for success in college and in life[21]. There are currently 162 KIPP schools in 20 states and the District of Columbia serving more than 58,000 students (and counting). More than 88 percent of their students are from low-income families and eligible for the federal free or reduced-price meals program, and 95 percent are African American or Latino. Many students have experienced (and continue to experience) significant trauma and discord in their families and neighborhoods. Nationally, more than 93 percent of KIPP middle school students have graduated high school, and more than 82 percent of KIPP alumni have gone on to college. The program is largely founded on character building, which focuses on seven very predictive, highly researched traits: zest, grit, self-control, optimism, social intelligence, curiosity, and gratitude. What these educators found, as well as many others, is that traits such as gratitude can be taught, even to those who seem to have many reasons not to be thankful. Qualities such as gratitude not only foster personal responsibility and achievement, but also teach youth that much of their success depends on the well-being of a larger team.

On Father's Day 2010, our family set off on a morning bike ride. What started out as a fun day turned into horror when our daughter plunged off a precipice after losing control on a local trail. A rock crushed through her forehead just under the helmet. When she stood up, we realized that a hole had opened into the inner covering of her brain. Amy and I thought we might be saying goodbye. But, many extraordinary things happened on her way to being blessed with an emergency craniotomy in the wee hours of the following day—her 4th birthday. This morning, I walked by her room as she slept soundly after another frenetic day at the Schroeder household. The seven titanium plates and the scars remain, although somewhat faded over the years. I am reminded that she could easily have not been with us. Yet I know we would have been asked to carry on, even joyously, without her. Years removed from that Father's Day morning, I am not grateful for the experience nor do I hope to ever encounter a similar one again. But I am tremendously thankful for the insight and the gratitude it has provided.

It was not the dawn flooding the bay with splendor
which woke Frederick...rather it was a gradual

awareness of flaming words...all around him—living things that carried him down wide rivers and over mountains and across spreading plains. Then it was people who were with him—black men, very tall and big and strong. They turned up rich earth as black as their broad backs; they hunted in forests; some of them were in cities, whole cities of black folks. For they were free; they went wherever they wished; they worked as they planned. They even flew like birds, high in the sky. He was up there with them, looking down on earth which seemed so small. He stretched his wings. He was strong. He could fly. He could fly in a flock of people...

—Excerpt from *There Was Once a Slave*, by Shirley Graham

Part V: Meaning & Transcendence

Frederick Augustus Washington Bailey (later known as Frederick Douglass) was born a slave circa 1818. After being separated from his mother as infant, and later from his grandmother, he was sent to live in a plantation nearby only to be eventually placed into servitude with the Auld family in Baltimore. Despite a Maryland law prohibiting slaves from being taught to read, Frederick acquired early literary skills from a member of his master's family. But after acquiring further abilities and gaining recognition as a teacher himself, he was sent to local farmer who had the repute of being a "slave breaker." Frederick barely survived one particular beating that left him bleeding and near death in the woods. With the aid of two mysterious individuals, Frederick found himself in a moment of transcendence as described above, eventually on his way to freedom. His life would become one of great meaning as social reformer, orator, writer, and leader of the movement to abolish slavery for good.

For all who suffer, like Mr. Douglass, meaning must first come through survival. But at some point, a question emerges about whether distress and misery mean more than the pain one feels. An inquiry of transcendence appears. In a study of those affected by severe childhood trauma, surviving is defined as "to continue to exist or simply to stay alive" (pg. 256)[22]. For those who survive, they are able to find a way through each day that comes, but past trauma still exerts significant control over their life. But with those who transcend, there is a sense of rising above the ordinary physical and psychological state. Although traumatic experiences themselves may remain as definitive and directive circumstances in a person's life, transcendence provides an escape to a more meaningful, and often joyful existence.

It appears that in the journey towards transcendence there first comes a growing awareness that something more exists beyond the palpable struggle. In the study mentioned above, awareness was generally followed by a sense of resiliency, of fighting back and persevering against the many restrictive forces, including self-blame. As noted in a study of male survivors of childhood sexual abuse, resiliency partially involves constructing a cognitive framework that makes sense of a traumatic past[23]. This may include a recognition of the perpetrator's own struggles; it may be an acknowledgment that being mistreated does not mean the victim received "punishment" for being a bad person. Gradually for many, acceptance of what has happened, and of roles that others may have played, seeps in. At

190

some point, opportunities for forgiveness emerge. It seems the avenue of forgiveness then becomes directly tied to helping others, resulting in a posited "altruism born of suffering"[24]. For many, this all leads to a greater sense of purpose and meaning, often through spiritual endeavors.

Although trends suggest stages towards transcendence, the reality is that "making meaning" of suffering runs a varied course. However, three themes seem to apply: meaning through reason and understanding, meaning through action, and meaning through spirituality[25]. For those who find meaning through action, a "survivor mission" often involves creating purpose by channeling negative energy they feel into actions that matter, and can help save others from perpetration. Some find meaning in slowly removing the intrapsychic barbs. Some even find meaning in creative and artistic endeavors.

But is true meaning a fleeting, far-reaching reality? Some philosophers have suggested that few ever reach its promised shores; others believe it is essential even to survive. It seems this paradox cannot be. In a recent study, two researchers from Missouri set out to address these two questions: Is life truly meaningful at all, and if so, is it available to many or just a few?[26] Their extensive review and analysis suggested that life is, in fact, both very meaningful and abundant at a high level. And not just for those who superficially seem to have few struggles. Polls taken by those hospitalized with alcoholism, in cocaine recovery programs, over the age of 85, and those critically ill all said the same thing: life has great importance.

So if life is in fact so full of meaning, why is it that only a limited number of people indicate they are thriving in their daily lives? Studies have generally noted that less than 1 in 5 people in the United States report that they are flourishing. More report that they are languishing or even worse[27]. It is understandable that many people struggle greatly due to adverse experiences. But often those with the worst experiences don't report the most distress, and those with only minor difficulties seem to barely get by.

Beyond all other issues, three restraining personal factors repeatedly seem at play. One is the reality of self-blame, as contrasted with self-worth. While the former is associated with a sense of unworthiness and helplessness, the latter speaks of an acute mindfulness of the value that each of us have. Self-worth should not be confused with narcissism and/or inflated self-esteem. Narcissism involves the attribution that the individual alone is responsible for blessings granted and accolades attained. Self-worth recognizes that much of what produces meaning and happiness is acquired from beyond. Although we recognize that all of us commit mistakes and transgressions, the manifestation of self-worth invokes an understanding that each person is worth that of another, only expressed in a unique way. A leader may influence by her life. A helper may influence by his heart. Sufferers can influence by their witness. But all lives can have great meaning, much of which will always be beyond our poor powers to perceive. So it seems the only thing more tragic than when people feel discarded by the world is when they are discarded by themselves.

These ideas form a converging point of trauma focused cognitive-behavioral therapy (TF-CBT). When creating painstaking narratives of a traumatic event(s), individuals come to understand how to disentangle deep-seeded beliefs of self-blame, and reframe these with realistic attributions and acknowledgements which stress that many factors associated with the trauma(s) were at play. Trauma starts looking less like an affirmation of an individual's self-loathing; it becomes more like an encounter(s) to be better understood and departed from.

Secondly, research has consistently found that attitudes must be accompanied by daily practices and environmental adjustments to provide a framework for a happier existence. The horrors of trauma must be directly, and repeatedly, contradicted by habits of contentment. If anxiety-provoking flashbacks persist, positive experiences must allow for new memories to be formed. If hatred stews incessantly, then regular acts of joy and giving must replace. If heightened arousal remains, then daily measures of calming practices and peaceful encounters must move in. Hard as it seems, unfair as it is, if joy and contentment are desired, somehow that rock must erode away.

But beyond self-blame and habitual practices, it appears that one factor looms above all. This issue serves to bury many people in the catacombs of their own selves and enables generations of trauma to ensue. It is the factor of fear. Born of stigmatization or alienation or condemnation or complete objectification, the dictatorial nature of fear knows no bounds. In order to find meaning and transcendence, one must again find hope, and faith, and ultimately love. Fear once again prevents love. Without love of some kind, encountering regular joy becomes unlikely, and distress is always a window away.

† † † †

From a young age, many of us were taught to pray and forgive others when we were worried and distressed. Some of us learned that helping people not only makes them feel better, but also us. If we were fortunate, we found out that we could channel negative energy into exercise and other physical endeavors, and gradually learn how to think more constructively as a means of reducing our angst. But very often when you hear people talk about these endeavors, all of which can serve to reduce distress, an artificial division seems to emerge as if they stem from separate beings and from a different Source.

Few, if any, would challenge the notion that prayer was given to us as a divine means of reducing our fears, among other functions such as praise, honor, and seeking forgiveness. No doubt this is regarded as God's domain. Some may argue similarly with helping others, although the percentages would likely decrease who agree with this notion. But if people were asked whether channeling energy into physical endeavors, or reframing negative thoughts, for the purpose of "not being afraid" was of a divine design, I suspect that there would be quite a dissension, especially as psychology and medicine have often not been considered friends of the faithful.

Yet this seems strange, almost as if we have allowed the compartmentalizations and specializations in our own life to blind us to the fact that once again, our being is only His being of design if we infuse wholeness. Whatever serves to reduce our distress in a holy and happy way can have only one Source; otherwise, we are of multiple designers. In order to fully understanding the capacity that each entity holds, it seems we must consider just what role He plays in it all, and just why a particular

194

facet of our being exists. This seems no truer than when it comes to how we feel each day.

When it comes to the time-honored, research-driven methods of turning distress into joy, we begin and end with a simple idea: The Savior of the World used these very techniques throughout his ministry. Although as God he would not have needed their restorative effects, his complete humanness suggests he was prone to the toll that stress can cause just as his followers were. Repeatedly, he speaks of the importance of forgiveness, advising all to forgive those who transgress against them. In the ultimate act of forgiveness after his crucifixion, he utters those timeless words, "Forgive them father, they know not what they do." (Luke 23:34).

But Jesus did not just forgive. He repeatedly sought opportunities to channel His energy, through prayer, fasting, movement, and solitude, presumably not only in obedience and thanks to God, but to deal with the difficult circumstances that He faced. As He increasingly helped others through His preaching and His healing, it should be noted that early in His ministry, He left Nazareth as He "was not able to perform any mighty deeds there... amazed at their lack of faith" (Mark 6:5-6). Like us, we wonder if even Jesus needed to know that He *mattered* to others in His desire to help them. Yet as His works began to spread throughout the surrounding land, so did the gratitude He expressed for all He was given. Whether it was for the rising of Lazarus, the multiplication of the loaves and fishes, or even gratitude prior to His greatest moment of suffering, giving thanks remained a constant part of His expression. Ultimately, through all of these efforts, Christ sought transcendence in God from a world that was often full of distress and suffering.

It is easy to think of Jesus in divine terms. He raised the dead. He healed the sick. He resurrected. But when we consider Him in human terms, we must consider that the daily opportunities we have to heal were also granted to Him. No doubt that He helped, and forgave, and gave thanks *for* the people of His time, and *for* us today. But is it possible that it was also for Him, so that through divinely orchestrated actions done in very human ways, His distress also turned to joy?

17

What Our Emotions Are Trying to Tell Us

When you are through learning, you are through
—John Wooden

They are as certain as death and taxes. They dominate our life. They often fluctuate minute by minute, hour by hour, year by year. They are a fabric of our very inner most being. Billions of dollars are spent every year in marketing to lure us in through them. Words describing them show up everywhere in our languages. Even in our sleep, we experience them. They often consume us. They are responsible for some of the most magnificent creations and the most atrocious deeds. They remain with us from the very beginning of life and only leave us when we are gone from this earth. They are our feelings and emotions.

From an evolutionary standpoint, our feelings have always played a critical role in our survival. They have guided us toward life-preserving actions and away from things that threaten our existence. They are vital to sustaining us as a species. They are necessary in understanding much of who we are, whether we are eight or eighty.

From the simplest of perspective, four basic emotions form a foundation of our daily experience. They are fear, anger, sadness, and happiness. They are known by many different names, but all are identifiable even by very young children. Three out of four are perceived to be negative. Only happiness is sought as an end in itself. The rest must be reasoned with, which implies that the thoughts associated with each feeling may be just as important as the feeling itself. No one seeks to be angry, or sad, or fearful, but instead we wrestle with each as we seek a happier resolution.

Beyond these four basic emotions, we can further distinguish between different categories of feelings although there's certainly grey area. The first category involves emotions seemingly meant for immediate activation, what we will call *lower-order* emotions. These include anxiety, fear, rage, and euphoria, among others. Recent research has indicated that when these activating emotions are not effectively addressed (especially at young age), they seem to create a chronic state of inflammation in the body. This not only can lead to bad choices and bad moods. It also seems to create a greater risk for diseases, such as cardiovascular, cancer and autoimmune conditions that may not manifest until decades later. These emotional states were never intended to last a long time.

The second category of emotions is what we will call *higher-order* emotions. Not surprisingly these take much longer to register in the body than the first. Some seem to welcome a chronic course, and the more they are present, the better outcomes we see. These are the emotions of love, trust, empathy, compassion, and others. Other *higher-order emotions,* such as depression, despair, helplessness, and apathy are unfortunate holdovers from activators never resolved.

So it makes us wonder that if the largest portion of basic feelings are negative and if the purpose of these emotions is not the feelings themselves, then they must be there for a reason. The issue is that this logic often does not seem to coincide with our actions. Instead of discerning the reason for our feelings, our first response is often one of avoidance or denial. We often seek to repress these emotions, to squelch their intensity, to distract ourselves away from them. There is a reason that anti-depressants are a thirteen billion dollar and counting industry. There is a reason that neuropsychiatric disorders prove far and away the most common cause of disability and premature death in the world. Emotions can be excruciating to deal with. They can seem overwhelming and exhausting. They can wreak havoc not only on our state of mind, but also the state of our body. Who can blame us for wanting to just get rid of them in any way possible?

However, when people offer helpful ideas, we often reject them because accepting them would acknowledge that others are not solely responsible for our struggles, that we are part of the problem. We want something or someone to simply take the horrible feelings away, not suggest that the solution may lie within our willingness and commitment to change. Admitting that our pride, the root of all vices, may be rendering us immobile acknowledges the most difficult reality of all: all change starts from within. And so we often run from this, seeking out evidence that would support how we have been wronged, avoiding that which may not confirm our worst fears. In psychology, we call this *confirmatory bias*. It is the process by which we consciously or unconsciously seek out experiences or ideas that support what we believe while discarding or ignoring those that do not. The potential travesty of this bias is that it may serve to lead us to *our* truth, not necessarily *the* truth. The more this happens over time, and the more we seek to avoid acknowledging the true emotional turmoil from within, the harder change becomes.

But for a second, let's return to the evolutionary principle. Anthropologists universally agree that emotions are there for a reason. If sometimes they seem excessive, they certainly are not superfluous, and they carry important messages that we need to heed.

Let's take anxiety. Though anxiety disorders are the most common psychological diagnosis in adults and kids, all anxiety is not bad. Some is actually very good, not to mention informative. Before we are quick to find ways to medicate or avoid our anxiety, we might want to ask the question: Is my anxiety telling me something? Avoiding anxiety on the short-term feels great because it takes the discomfort away, but in the long-term, it can rob us in many ways. It may take away the opportunity to improve a skill, such as public speaking, that opens doors; keep us from overcoming a fear – of dogs, for example, that allows us to move about more freely; or lead us to avoid confronting a thorny disagreement, that would allow us to get closer to a friend; or leave us susceptible to bad habits and addictions to relieve unresolved worry. The reality is that the avoidance of anxiety may not be the best pathway, even though it *certainly feels* like the best choice.

The same goes for all other emotions. Sometimes our fears are telling us to get away quickly, such as with an oncoming train. Sometimes our anger is telling us we need to step away and cool off before doing something we might regret. Many times our feelings are actually giving us an opportunity to recognize a weakness or an imbalance in our life. But whether emotions serve as an entreaty for engagement or retreat, they only enable progress if we willingly listen to what they're telling us.

In theory, this idea seems rather straightforward. In practice, it is anything but. The idea of facing our feelings head on is a deeply uncomfortable proposition. It means we must tolerate uncertainty. It means we must cope with awkwardness, even in our own mind. Facing our fears is universally taught as the precursor to courage, but understanding our feelings and acting on what they tell us is real fortitude.

There are a few big challenges that we must face. First is the acknowledgment that the way we have been doing things may not be the way we really *want* or *should* be doing things. Second is knowing that we may have to seek out forgiveness, including from ourselves, as well as others. Few enjoy this, but the result can be liberating. Finally, we must be willing to embrace the idea that the greatest rewards come from the most difficult struggles.

If we can embrace these challenges, then the potential to learn from our emotions can yield a satisfaction greater than we can imagine. But all of this is only possible if we allow for a few basic things when we feel an emotion coming on. One is time. Without it, it is impossible to learn. Two is the willingness to tolerate discomfort without quickly seeking to get rid of the feeling itself. Three is openness to the insight that may come, even if it impels us to take a different direction. Four is action, even if it is in the smallest degree. Regarding anxiety, it has been shown that the best treatment consists of gradual exposure with response prevention. In other words, it is taking small steps (e.g., looking at pictures of snakes in a book) while using calming techniques (e.g., deep breathing) before we move onto something more challenging. Without action of any kind, our feelings serve to stagnate us, often for decades.

So if we are a species of emotions, and emotions serve a clear function, then we owe it to ourselves to pay close attention to what they are saying. We do this when our engine light goes on (or at least we should). We do this when the smoke alarm goes off. We do this when we hear a siren coming down the road. Why wouldn't we do this when we find ourselves anxious for the umpteenth time in the same situation? It seems that if we are stuck with them, we might as well use them to grow and create deeper meaning in our life. Just because the saber tooth tiger is extinct doesn't mean we shouldn't take action when the hair is bristling up our back and our muscles suddenly go tight.

† † † †

We began this pursuit of the four dimensions of our being with the subject of fear and anxiety. Back we come to this subject and that of varied emotions that we feel every day. To feel is certainly to be human, but to be defined by our feelings can be dangerous and irrational. In fact, in the world of cognitive-behavioral therapy, "emotional reasoning" is identified as a cognitive distortion that occurs when we automatically believe that what we feel must be true. If we feel like an idiot, then we must *be* an idiot. If we feel unloved, then we must *be* unloved.

But the irony of emotional reasoning is that it doesn't just apply to negative emotions. Just because we feel smart doesn't necessarily mean we *are* smart. Just because we feel in love doesn't automatically mean we *are* loved. In either instance, whether of a positive or negative variety, we are impelled to consider the context and consistency with which they occur. For example, just because we feel smart at a particular task doesn't necessarily mean that we are smart at many other tasks, or even the task at hand. Many a singers and crooners feel quite melodic in the shower, only to be horribly off-key under the lights. Not only must we consider just how the place where we feel something may significantly affect our perception, but we also must be aware of how consistent our experiences are. A golfer may feel confident that he or she is quite skilled at a home course, a place this person has played thousands of times. Yet suddenly they might find their confidence waning significantly after a few holes on a links of a new variety. But truly great golfers, no matter where they play, will find a way to play well on golf courses of all kinds.

Beyond context and consistency, the measure of a feeling is how it reflects upon virtue. If we really want to know what a particular feeling is telling us to do, then we must ask ourselves where it intersects with a virtuous reality. While feelings fluctuate considerably, virtues remain staunch, even in the face of significant pressure and strain. For example, if I come home angry after work repeatedly, and displace my anger upon my family and my pets, then it behooves me to first recognize the factors of context and consistency, but then consider a few basic questions. Are my reactions just, here and at work? Am I exhibiting fortitude in handling challenging situations in a transparent, unselfish way? Am I acting temperately when I feel rage coming on? And are my decisions prudent for what matters most, or am I finding myself investing in trivial and potentially harmful endeavors? In this situation, anger can become a tool of awareness and motivation, but only if I consider my unrelenting anger as a useful agent, not a perpetual catharsis. Emotions without the backdrop of virtue are as useless and uninformed as a cat going in search of his tail.

None of this is an attempt to divorce feelings and emotions from the inner fabric of our human experience. As I noted in the reflection, they run through us and in us like an ever-flowing river. But when we speak of lower-order emotions, we must recognize that they are fleeting, and often not reliable unless we take stock of just what they might mean. When the subject of "higher-order emotions" arises, what we quickly realize is that *emotion* is probably not even the correct word. Love, trust, admiration, and the like are truly more a state of will and grace than they are feeling. To experience them in their fullness is to experience them in toil and suffering, not just bliss and harmony. But to get there, we must constantly be in a state of will, both of our God-given will and the graceful will that He bestowed on us.

The duality of will that is needed first springs forth when we realize that in order to reach a higher order, we must work through a lower rung. That is what St. John exhorted us to do when he said that fear prevents love. In order to find ourselves elevated in love, we must first find ourselves trudging through the thick, clingy mud of fear, anxiety, and other unwanted emotions. Effort really is the mechanism of elevation, but love, just like happiness, often is difficult to pursue if we are simply pursuing its pleasure while avoiding its pain. True love requires true vulnerability. True vulnerability requires that we are continually recognizing our shortcomings, our faults, our irrational beliefs and feelings, and taking those steps needed to purify ourselves of all these experiences, even if for brief, fleeting moments. There, when the proverbial dust clears, we may suddenly realize that love is waiting for us. Come inside after a bone-chilling day spent doing your best to remain industrious and keep unwanted despair and negativity at bay. What you may find is a true love almost forgotten of the simple warmth that your home brings.

Imagine for a few minutes that we could suspend reality; Imagine at least briefly, we really did regard emotions of all kinds as an entry point to a more authentic reality where how we felt informed us, not despaired us. What if a funeral that day attended by many loved ones evoked not only genuine mourning, but also varied feelings of contemplation, anxiety, and fervor that lead to each attendee making real, sustained changes in their lives? What if I walked into a store today and felt panicked for the hundredth time, but this time thought to myself, "What could I really do to reduce my fears not just for me, but so my kids grow up in a better way?" And then I sought out further support and acted on these initial inclinations. What if in my sorrow about hearing about local children in need, I stopped finding reasons I could not help, but instead took a few steps to make it possible? Obviously, I recognize that complications would ensue if we took every emotion seriously as sometimes feelings are best observed, not acted upon. Still, the simple point is what if we took seriously the inherent messages of our feelings just as we did the requirements of our work, or the maintenance of our leisure? Many might be quick to invest thousands of dollars and significant time in getting a boat in hopes that it provides much enjoyment and relaxation. It may. But would we be just as quick to invest the time and money required to improve our emotional state, even there was less assurance that the effort would lead to fruition?

I am not suggesting that we all head to a therapist for weekly sessions although sometimes, the money spent here might be a formative place to start. But I am suggesting that it is due time that we consider our emotional pursuits as a religious endeavor, not to mention a physical reality and a social agent. Very often, we are tempted to pray for miracles. "God, please take this away from me." As I mentioned before, though, we might find ourselves in a position where God seems to say that the miracle happened when we were given the mind and body to handle much strife. I do believe that many times, God puts the "ball back in our court." His grace never leaves, but if it is true that His Spirit lives within us, our body and the mind must be willing to allow a miracle to happen, even if the miracle is simply that we willfully take a step towards emotional progress not previously taken.

On the night in which Christ prayed in the garden, he faced a final temptation. It was the temptation of allowing his fear to prevent the ultimate love. When he spoke to his Almighty Father, he pleaded with him, "My Father, if it is possible, let this cup pass from me; yet, not as I will, but as You will." (Matthew 26:39). In what many consider as his most human moment, he acknowledged what he was feeling. He did not deny that he was scared. Then, recognizing the horrors that lie ahead, he asked for help of the most Ultimate Kind.

At this moment, as an emotional, feeling human being, something remarkable happened. His lower-order emotion subsumed itself into a higher order will. Actually, two wills. His will and His will. For when he uttered the statement "yet, not as I will, but as You will", He in essence stated that His love for God, His Father, would overrule the emotions he felt so that ultimately His Father's will would prevail. He sensed that the final spiritual conquest was the confrontation and elimination of his own fear so that the perfection of Love could be realized. Before God's love could be complete, it seemed that his fear must pass away to the ages. As he told his disciples, "Keep watching and praying that you may not enter into temptation. The spirit is willing, but the flesh is weak." (Matthew 26:41) He knew what his emotions were telling him, and he knew where it must lead, and that he must let go. But He was yet to understand why.

18

Why Oh Why?

From noon onward, darkness came over the whole land until three in the afternoon. And about three o'clock Jesus cried out in a loud voice, "*Eli, Eli, lema sabachthani?*" which means, "My God, my God, why have you forsaken me?"

—Matthew 45:46

It is one of the most common questions in the English language. In my office, it is often loaded with more emotion than any other. *Why? Why* does my child do that? *Why* is he that way? *Why* did this happen? Some questions are huge. Some seem rather trivial. Psychologists who focus on behavioral change similarly work with parents to understand *why* a behavior occurs so that we can teach children a better method to achieve a particular goal. But too often, we as parents get so bogged down on the question of *why*, and never move onto *what is next*.

Some ways back, I found myself in the office with a mother of a child diagnosed with a moderate intellectual disability (previously categorized as mental retardation). Like up to forty percent of children with an intellectual disability, there was no clear medical reason for the deficits that this child displayed. Years of appointments had left this mother feeling disappointed and discouraged that nothing could explain what had happened. As we sat there, tears rolled down her face as she continued to wonder aloud if there was some medical test or genetic screening that could provide an answer. The mental anguish and physical strain from this unresolved issue had taken its toll.

Years ago, researchers Camille Wortman and Roxanne Silver performed a series of pioneering studies[1]. They asked thousands of people to explain how they had dealt with tragic events in their lives, whether it is the death of a loved one, incest, chronic illness, or other circumstances. Three general groups seemed to emerge. Those who had come to a simple, causal explanation for the tragedy had generally done well. Those who had never looked for a clear explanation, but simply moved forward seemed to also remain resilient. But those who had continued searching for the answers to "*Why* did this happen?" and "*Why* me?", and never found a satisfactory reason, struggled the most. In some ways, they had never moved on. The authors noted that although causal thinking is critical to our species, it can lead to serious hardships when dealing with tragedy. Continued searching may only result in further heartache, failed relationships, and the loss of health and well-being.

From an early age, many of us began to form a vision of how our life was going to look someday. We saw our children growing up, going to college, and getting married. We imagined ourselves growing comfortably old with our spouse. We envisioned our careers unfolding in particular ways. It all seemed so clear until misfortune and suffering came. The purpose that once was evident suddenly lacked clarity. Finding meaning seemed impossible. Then came a choice. Either accept a new vision, one that was never intended, or cling to the one that had shattered fully.

Forgetting ourselves for the moment, this is where the question of *why* becomes critical for our children. No one is discounting how excruciating it is to lose a loved one before their time. No one questions how painful a divorce can be or how frustrating it is to lose a job. The situations seem completely unfair. They always will be from a worldly point of view. However, when we cannot get beyond *why*, it seems to immobilize us.

In the absence of clear answers, we sometimes forget *we can* do things every day to move forward. For starters, we can put effort into having good relationships with each other. We can provide regular, consistent routine at home. We can provide our children with ongoing opportunities for exercise, good dietary options, and appropriate sleep habits while minimizing those influences that we know are not good for them. We can communicate with them regularly even if they do not respond in the way we desire. We can take care of our own health and well-being, knowing that we cannot give to our children what we do not have. We can learn from others who have found ways to transcend pain. These people can become our best friends. We can learn to love the new goals that life may unexpectedly bring. We can work to find meaning within our struggle. And at the times we are only left with suffering, we can offer it to something beyond ourselves. These are things that all of us can benefit from, including our children. Someday, maybe sooner than expected, they may also be faced with the question of *why*.

If this sounds like common sense, it is. But often when things are really despairing, it is too easy to forget that not knowing *why* does not mean we cannot have hope. It may just mean that our hopefulness that day comes from walking to the front door instead of staying in bed.

I spend much of my days working with kids on the autism spectrum. They can be some of the most extraordinary and frustrating children alike. I have come to notice something interesting that is certainly not exclusive to this population. The progress and adjustment of these children seems to have as much, or even more, to do with the parents' abilities to provide for the family's basic needs as it does with specific interventions and treatments. Both are certainly important. But one without the other creates a tenuous situation. In the end, it seems that parents who learn to balance both are the ones whose children have the best outcomes.

In 1997, at the age of 92, Holocaust survivor Viktor Frankl passed away forty-five years after he was liberated from the concentration camps. His parents, brother, and wife never made it out. By the time he had died, his memoir *Man's Search for Meaning* had sold over ten million copies and been translated into twenty-four languages. He received an average of over twenty letters a day during his final years mostly thanking him for changing the lives of those who had read his book. His family members would continue to receive letters after he had passed. Logotherapy, developed by Frankl as a means of treating a number of psychological conditions, became known the world over. It is based on the idea that life has meaning, even in the worst situations. We are always free to seek out this meaning. Frankl believed there are three basic ways to find this meaning: service to others, personal encounter or true experiencing, and our attitude towards unavoidable suffering. He was quoted as saying, "Everything can be taken from a man but one thing: the last of the human freedoms—to choose one's attitude in any given set of circumstances." Along the way, it seems that his life became little about *why* and much about finding meaning in *what came next.*

Each of us, in small or great ways, will be forced to deal with difficult situations that do not make sense. Many of us will find that this takes us through the intersection of will and faith. Regardless of where *why* gets us, it seems that we must never forget that each day provides a renewed opportunity to ask *what is next.* It is not that we shouldn't forever be open to new insights that bring clarity to our *why* questions. But it's just that, in whatever way possible, we must work to accept *what is,* and push forward with whatever *is to be.* Otherwise, we may be missing the opportunities that lie all around us to see a new light in an otherwise dark place.

† † † †

I wonder just how long Jesus knew that he would die on the cross. It is easy to speculate that once his ministry began, he was endowed with a sense that his conventional work would end quickly. Maybe, though, this vision would not come to him until later. We do not know. Regardless, at the point in which it became clear he must die, it seems the "why question" probably never left him. As he was being scourged, and beaten, and forced to carry his cross, I can't help but think that he harbored this question throughout. It was only in His final moments that this lack of understanding could be publicly heard, in what could be described as His last moment of authentic human vulnerability. From there, he would die and be risen, and

His mission on this earth would be become clear, and His uncertainty would be put to rest.

Meanwhile, the disciples must have found themselves questioning everything in the same way. They had given up their livelihood and their reputations to follow this small-town preacher. Now with his death, all seemed to be lost and they scattered across the land, fearful that they too would face a similar fate. Despair and futile attempts at understanding followed, and we can only surmise that they dreamt of their former lives.

Yet in the midst of the unanswered question, signs of *what is next* emerged all over the land. Jesus himself endured torture, crucifixion, and death without having clear answers. After His apostles saw their Risen Lord, they too began to consider that the mission had not failed, and small seeds of messianic work began to sprout even though fear remained. Ten days after Christ left this earth for good, the Spirit descended on them like tongues of fire. Fear dissolved, and what happened next changed the world for good.

As we near the end of our journey here, we stop for a moment to consider the unresolved issues in our own lives. Human nature dictates that all of us will look for answers in some ways, at some times. The question first becomes, "What will I do if I find the answers I seek?" If the mother I described had come to understand just why her daughter had the disability, I wonder just what that would have done for her? Would it have relieved the guilt she might have felt? Would the answer have given her solace that came with not being left in the dark, or knowing that others have experienced the same? I wonder. I know that we all look for answers as if they hold keys to a solution. Still, sometimes I sense they are often just another door into unanswered questions and unfulfilled wishes.

Yet, the message of *why* is once again a message of effort, of will, of faith, and of grace. Just as Christ and the disciples, and those resilient folks in the studies, taught us about tragedy, so we must never forget that the answers never lie in the knowledge of the past. Certainly, it can be reassuring to have clarity about why things happened. But unless this knowledge leads us to a path of self-improvement and a path of serving God over ourselves, this knowledge will lead to no wisdom at all.

All suffering has meaning, but meaning runs straight through those four dimensions like flowing waters tunneling underground. If tragedy leads us to repair or seek out new relationships for the better, then a spring begins to wear away at solid rock. If despair leads us to renewal through increased health and well-being, then gradually a small underground river can emerge. If depression leads to a commitment to gratitude, forgiveness, and ultimately psychological well-being, then suddenly that river bursts into the open landscape and begins to change the topography forever. And if hopelessness spurs a realization that all is not lost if He is gained, then a grand canyon emerges one day. There, we find ourselves in an ancient river full of life-giving water, staring up at the soaring canyon walls, surrounded by our brothers and sisters wondering just how we ever got here. Just as Viktor Frankl never let *why* be the answer he sought, so we must set our sights on *what is next* even if we fear the valley of the shadow of death.

What is next never happens, though, unless we embrace *what is now*. We have heard this from countless theologians and philosophers, but truly the greatest

214

robbery occurs when the moments we have now are stolen away, often by ourselves. The future contains us in our hopelessness. The past defines us in our helplessness. The present gives us our happiness. We can talk about fond memories and upcoming excitement, but these only come into fruition when we are present enough to make memories worth having and perceive possibilities worth effusing. So frequently, though, despair and mundaneness rob us of simple pleasures and regular opportunities for contentment that really are available for all; some less obvious than others, but always available somehow. We are tempted to believe that joy and hope are only privy to the privileged. Then, we encounter barefoot kids in Haiti and warring tribes in Africa, and find that they are happier than we.

Tonight, as we wrapped up the celebration for our son, Noah, on the occasion of his fourth birthday, my father-in-law reminded me of this on a frigid evening. As a young kid Noah's age, every bathroom call for him meant a trip outside to the privy, even if the temperatures were below zero. As we were saying prayers of thanks together, my father-in-law gave gratitude that he got a chance to use the bathroom tonight and throughout the winter in a heated confine. Our kids have no reference point about just how much of a privilege this is. But he does. And many others in impoverished circumstances around the globe would love to know how it feels to use the bathroom indoors.

Every day we move forward, and not dwell on *why*, we must also make a conscious, willful effort to be in the now, and love in the now. We really have nothing else. It does not mean we shouldn't plan for the future, or reflect on the past. But it means that we can't give away our heart and soul to either. When we emotionally find ourselves tied to before or after, our well for this moment drains until we are left with waters that once ran deep, but now are shallow; capacities that once were large, but now are small; love that once seemed real, but now is fleeting. The question then becomes, just what happiness are we seeking?

19

Just What Happiness Are We Seeking?

Those who are happy have their minds fixed on some object other than their own happiness
—John Stuart Mill

In the 1950's, a group of psychologists began to write and promulgate theories and ideas related to the pursuit of happiness and flourishing. Carl Rogers, Abraham Maslow, and a few others among them felt that for a long time, psychology had been consumed with what could go wrong instead of what could go right. As Martin Seligman noted decades later in the first sentence of his book, *Authentic Happiness*, "For the last half century psychology has been consumed with a single topic only—mental illness." In doing so, the field had been marred with a lack of recognition that people often find ways of contentment, resiliency, and meaning, even in the face of difficult obstacles.

The idea put forth was not a new one. For millennium, traditions of many kinds have spoken of this pursuit. The Israelites believed that happiness came in response to following the commands and rules put forth by Yahweh. The Greeks sought contentment through logic and analysis. Jesus and His message has always been the source of joy for Christians. In Islam, happiness comes from a "contented heart" that can be found in the remembrance and pleasure of God himself. Even many of a western existence seek out hedonistic practices in the idea that pleasure is the source of happiness.

The search for happiness is as ubiquitous as water and soil, yet the means and ideas for achieving it seem varied and contrary. Any pursuit for the good life must then ask, "Just what happiness are we seeking?" Because the term happiness has such a wide breadth, any discussion of this matter must first define just what is meant by this word. Martin Seligman proposes that there are three major "routes" to happiness: pleasure and positive emotion (the pleasant life), engagement (the engaged life), and meaning (the meaningful life)[1]. How we choose to seek out happiness in one or multiple areas may differ, but most people's practices and pursuits find themselves in at least one of these areas. Further research by Seligman and colleagues found that those who reported being most satisfied with their life were those who sought out experiences through all three routes, with a heavier emphasis towards the engaged and meaningful life[2].

But what is particularly intriguing is that although routes and practices may differ, research of peoples and cultures across the world find remarkable similarity in one area: virtue. Regardless of race, creed, practice, or experience, people consistently report that virtue remains virtue. Six universal virtues emerge. They are wisdom and knowledge, courage, humanity, justice, temperance, and transcendence. Within these six virtues are 24 character strengths, also endorsed across the world. For example, courage is composed of authenticity, bravery, persistence, and zest while temperance is composed of forgiveness, modesty, and prudence[3]. Available to all, exclusive to none, these virtues and strengths run like an undercurrent through our world, and into another.

In light of this, we must stop to ponder again. "Just what happiness are we seeking, and are we seeking it for now, later, and/or eternity?" And if we could find pleasure, engagement, and meaning through the pursuit of virtue, which is available and important to all, would this further guide us towards a particular pathway? It would be hard work at times, for sure, but would it start to make this pursuit of happiness much less mystifying? For example, in being just, I could feel pleasure in making the right decision, engage with people in a gratifying way, and find meaning that my actions were the better ways, now and for years to come. In being courageous, I could experience joy through challenging endeavors, meet others in their own struggles, and do something that really matters to those I love. Through virtue, maybe I could find happiness—experienced in my mind, body, heart, and soul. Maybe I could. I can. I have.

But, just as this seems to be all of it, I wonder where my humanity meets His divinity. Then a figure appears, an itinerant in the distant desert, walking with sandals on his dusty feet and a simple robe upon his body. He is followed by a few, yet He is silent. He looks so simple. He seems so plain. Yet he knows anguish, sorrow, and fear. He has felt fatigue, pain, and tears. He has loved and has lost. Then He smiles. Have I not seen His face before? Do I not know who He is? He looks at me as if to say, "Do you not understand that I am the confluence of all that is holy, and happy, and whole?" In my weakness and my pride, I look away, even though somewhere in the silence of my soul, I know that He is who He is. But my disbelieving self swells, and reminds me just how improbable His story is. For if He was really just an infant, just a boy, just a man—a Savior born in swaddling clothes—then I can think of no story more astonishing than when He became like me. Still, I must continue on the trail because nothing else promises what He does. Everything else seems to fall short—so transient, so concrete. He proclaims that He is the way, and the truth, and the life; that no one comes to the Father but through Him. I must see. I must know. I must feel. I must love. Maybe it isn't *what* happiness I am seeking after all. Maybe it is *Whose*...

† † † †

I laid awake listening to the winds power through the woods. Rain splattered on the tent fly above my head. A bowing pine squeaked in the forest. Steve and I had come back to German Ridge, but this time my brother and five friends had joined us.

It was a brilliant, unseasonably warm January morning as the temperatures would eventually reach above 50 degrees Our Saturday trek would take us over seventeen miles of rugged, undulating terrain, with three miles left to hike out on Sunday morning. Three in our group were undergoing their inaugural backpacking experience. For one, it had been 25 years since the straps tightened around his shoulders. Collectively, eight wives and 21 kids (and one on the way) were back home. By the time the stories had been told and 11,000 feet of elevation change had been traversed, the happiness we had been seeking found its way past the soreness back home.

But I knew from her that our happiness would come in being desired and being loved—in a togetherness that was as simple as the touch that we beheld, in the sense that we belonged. Descending into the hollow, the silent truth revealed itself midst the browned, crackly leaves.

Mile one.

I knew that he desired knowledge and wisdom, and a sense that he mattered to those who would listen to his ideas and his ways. Sprung from calls of industry and ingenuity, he spoke of ways to reach a larger audience— those who yearned for direction in this noisy world. A flock of sparrows flew across the trail. Quietness ensued.

Mile four.

He told me that wanted renewed health and vigor, and to not succumb to the fatigue that tempted a more sedentary way. In his sadness over his family's declining health, he began to see more clearly how the gift of fitness was a precious key to contentment. A meadow suddenly opened itself on the edge of the forest.

Mile seven

It was beauty and transcendence that made his heart swell. Although tempted to take an easier route, he disciplined himself to stay the difficult course, to seek the narrow way. I strode behind him silently admiring his toil in the midst of uncertainty that lay and sadness in those departing soon. The sun reflected off the hillside onto the ridge above.

Mile nine

Beneath his smile, I sensed that he desired a permanent resurrection to a life not controlled by an addictive force. In the courage to improve and atone for his sins, temperance became a source of perpetual joy. It was not easy. Yet he smiled repeatedly in quietness as the pines swayed to meet him in consolation.

Mile eleven

Justice was his creed and in fairness he found solace. He had dedicated himself to the pursuit of a linear course in a quadrilateral world. Pleasant remembrances of his youth strode next to him as the semi-frozen brooks flowed anew.

Mile thirteen

A tired, achy warrior emerged. Although he desired rest, he yearned for respect and understanding in an early life marred by abuse and rage. In his humanity, he was in search of a mutual kindness that would become his contentment. The jagged rocks looming above resonated with him in their variegated state.

Mile seventeen

Crowded around a fire, warmth became our glee. Tales of youthful escapades and familial realities radiated over the crackling, flaming light as faces framed in simple belonging and natural wonders smiled across the way. Contentment buried extraordinary meaning in our ordinary day. We longed for all He could provide.

Mile eighteen

We had arisen from the spectacular gorge into our final ascent. It was oneness and wholeness that we sought once again as the cars came into view. In the last few steps of silence, each surrounded by the body of Christ, we would disperse just minutes later. They were waiting for us at home. None of us knew where next week would lead. But we had come. And we had walked, and shared, and laughed, and hugged, and smiled, and rested, and eaten, and in the shadow of that flickering light we had fallen asleep, only to be suddenly awoken and questioned about who we were and whether we had paid our dues. In the buffeting wind and the pouring rain, we answered the call and were left alone in the wilderness that we had sought, in the silence that asked whoooo?

Mile twenty...

Epilogue

Running to Him

Yet those who wait for the LORD will gain new strength; They will mount up with wings like eagles, They will run and not get tired, They will walk and not become weary.

—Isaiah 40:31

It was 22 degrees outside. The winter had been much colder than the last. The increased ice and snow had brought me to Helfrich Hills Golf Course more than expected as the other trails had been treacherous with frozen precipitation still clinging to their roots. But on this day, only a trace of snow lay on the unthawed, windswept hills as I began my long run. The sun had already begun its perpetual rise over the frozen landscape. I had settled into a quiet, rhythmic pattern that I hoped would maintain over the next few hours as the promise of a fifty mile run at Land between the Lakes beckoned in the spring time.

Just a couple of weeks before, it had been a much different story. My brother, Andrew, and I had joined up after a solitary hour on the slick, snow-covered roadways only to dive off into the deeply covered grounds of our beloved course. With our feet encased in plastic sacks underneath the quickly whitened sneakers, we made our way slowly downhill into the hidden fairway below. We would follow these unseen pathways just as we had done hundreds of times before, only this time the green was nowhere to be found. It was a plodding, at times strategic run that day as the six to eight inches of snow often drifted well over our ankles. It was an exercise in contrast, as we moved over slopes where others had been only to emerge into the virgin tundra where our footsteps remained alone.

That day, I finished my run alone only to find my way back to the course a week later. The snow had melted some, but the mild temperatures kept the sod underneath unexposed. This time, though, as I stepped out onto the hilly expanse, I realized it would be a much different day. Gone were the conditions of a week before in which my foot found the bottom through the soft, billowy snow. On this morning, each tenuous step was accompanied by a sinking, cracking feeling as the hardened blanket seemed to pull my foot downward in an uncertain embrace. Hours lay ahead of me, and as I carefully made my way down the twelfth fairway, I was uncertain whether this seemed to be a prudent course. Not only had the snow become a weakened, dicey foundation, but the sledders had created many minefields of miniature jagged peaks and valleys.

But as I turned towards the flat thirteenth fairway, I perceived something distinctly in the distance. Memories of the sledders and the walkers had cleared. There they were, alone in the whiteness that lay in front. I felt the emotion of love and gratitude sweep over me. I was not alone. Two sets of footprints, side by side, serpentined into the hills ahead as far as my eye could see. The day would turn out okay, of that I became sure. For just as the footprints would again leave me on the hilly parts, enveloped by the footprints of sledders gone past, our two sets of footprints would once again emerge again in the lonely flatlands.

Two weeks later, I came back for the third and last time that winter. Midst the chill of a below freezing morning, much of the brown and green had emerged and this day the footing would not be a concern. But as I turned onto the same thirteenth fairway and thought of the footprints that had melted away in front of me, I suddenly felt overtaken by a flood of transcendence. "Maybe it was just that simple," I perceived. Maybe all the analogous and metaphorical spiritual references I had heard over the years about running weren't just symbolic. Maybe the answer lay right in front of me, at the moment each of my feet hit the ground and returned to do the same, synthesized into the rhythm of my breathing and the angle of my body. Maybe running was part of the New Covenant, a mechanism for divinity on earth given to us by God, one available to everyone. Maybe we were born to run after all.

† † † †

In 2009, when Christopher McDougall published his widely acclaimed book *Born to Run,* it began as a personal journey to address his own running woes. The book weaved together stories about ultra-marathoners and barefoot runners and a mysterious tribe, the Tarahumara, known worldwide for their legendary running prowess. Nestled into a remote area of Mexico, these people had become renowned for superhuman feats of running that took them hundreds of miles through the Copper Canyons, only to eventually emerge in the public scene after the book's main character, Micah True (aka Caballo Blanco), convinced them to run in a few official races. Those who observed the Tarahumara runners deep in the races noted a uniqueness, something beyond character, something that could be best described as intense and uninhibited love. In the midst of the tale, McDougall describes the buzz created by two researchers, Dennis Bramble and Daniel Lieberman, who published a scintillating article in *Nature* in 2004 entitled *Endurance Running and the evolution of Homo*[1]. In the article, the writers detailed findings that suggested that humans had been purposefully evolved to run. They cited twenty-six features of the human body that seemed specifically designed for the purpose of endurance running with no other clear use.

The findings of this research were ground-breaking. For those who entertained this possibility, it raised further queries about why humans would have evolved this way. Bramble and Liberman, among others, speculated that it may have allowed them to participate in endurance hunting over long distances, eventually wearing down prey in order to provide for the types of proteins and fats needed to support the unique human anatomy. Interestingly, although many animals are much faster over short distances, the authors noted that humans possess endurance capabilities beyond that of most other larger species. Other theories suggested that the running adaptations may have improved scavenging capabilities as humans competed with other animals, such as hyenas, for needed food sources. But the theories stopped here. No assertions were made about possible psychological or spiritual benefits that underlay the ability to run.

Foregoing all of the speculation, though, was the tenet that humans seemed to possess an amazing capacity to run long-distances like few others, but one that McDougall posited had become misconstrued and disrupted by modern technology, including the current shoe. It had led many people to adopt unhealthy and unsustainable running patterns in ways that would forego their natural abilities. Moving away from centuries of running barefoot and minimal footwear, it seemed that newer designs had undermined the best running apparatus of all—the foot.

† † † †

At the age of forty-eight, Sister Madonna Buder had already lived a full life on the spiritual frontier. Raised in a wealthy, philanthropic St. Louis family, she heard a call early on that would defy her privileged upbringing. By fourteen years of age, she knew that God was summoning her to a life of service as a nun. Far away from the luxury of her home, and past the early wooing of her well-known suitors, including Thomas Dooley, she began her life of service despite the objections of her elders.

She had committed her life to various ministries, including that of prison care. But one day, she had a conversation with a priest, who suggested that she take up running. He told her that running harmonized the mind, spirit, and the body. So she picked up an old pair of tennis shoes, and took off, just a little at first, and by the end of a few weeks, her knees were swollen and she began to wonder what was going on. But gradually over time, her miles increased, and running led to cycling and swimming, and then all at once. She began to compete in triathlons and at the age of fifty-five, she entered in her first Ironman. Thirty years later, and more races than she could count, the *Iron Nun* had become a legend, and at the age of eighty-two, became the oldest human being to finish an Ironman before the midnight deadline.

In April of 2013, she found herself just a couple of miles from the finish line at the Boston Marathon. It had been a good race and she was reveling in the joy that came with once again being allowed to set new standards for humanity. But just as she settled in to those final miles, she heard an explosion and suddenly learned that a bomb had been detonated near the finish line. She would not finish the race that day. She later described to me the despair that she felt in being dispersed alone in the middle of these chaotic circumstances. But the following weekend, and the weekend after that, and the weekend after that, she kept her commitments to the triathlons so that, in her words (at an invocation before a subsequent race), so she like all could "...courageously vow to overcome evil by doing good." It was the little she could do to resurrect the horror that had occurred just days before. Each time, she strode across the finish line, reminding all that anything is possible with God. She once said, "If you can walk, you can run — just take one step at a time." When asked if she ever felt a "runner's high", she laughed and exclaimed that she didn't know what that was. It appeared that for her, running had always been an act of service.

Thirty years after Sister Madonna began her life of running, Marshall Ulrich found himself taking on yet another monumental task. In a life seemingly filled with endless adventures, and many peaks and valleys, he set off on the hardest adventure of all. He already climbed the tallest mountains on all seven continents, completed a Badwater quad (586 total miles that comprised the distance from Death Valley to Mount Whitney—four times each way) for his fiftieth birthday, and found himself in the winner's circle and the "He did *what*?" circuit more times than he could count. But his attempt to run across the United States in record time would bring on pain and heartache that questioned whether even he could accomplish his goal. But fifty-two days and 12 hours later, through often excruciating circumstances that led him to disown his own foot, he found himself on the steps of City Hall in New York City.

Years earlier, he had a chance conversation with Yiannis Kouros, a man who had once ran 188 miles in 24 hours. Ulrich described an experience one morning at the Badwater competition in which he remembered the sun rising behind him only to suddenly find himself observing his body from above, as if his spirit had left him moving below. In a seeming instant, he returned to his body only to realize that the sun was setting in front of him. Much of the day had passed without awareness. When he mentioned this to Kouros, the response was simple: it happens to me on a regular basis. As detailed in a 2006 article in the Running Times[2], *Sometimes he'll tell his crew not to interrupt him [Kouros] for an hour or two because "when someone is there to feed me, it brings me back to earth and I don't always want that during a race."*

† † † †

So what did all this mean? Well, for centuries, people had spoken of the "runner's high," but for a long time it seemed very difficult to find clear evidence that it actually existed. But this all changed, as detailed in a 2008 New York Times article entitled *Yes, Running Can Make You High*[3]. It told the story of researchers in Germany who found a way to measure the flood of endorphins that appears to occur when many run, as measured in comparison to neurological activity before and after a two hour jaunt by study participants. These endorphins are especially attached to areas of the brain associated with emotions, including the limbic system and prefrontal cortex. The change in endorphin patterns coincided with psychological report from the runners and observation of the athletes themselves, including their facial and mood patterns.

So if the euphoria is true, and is similar to other truly synergistic experiences, then further questions are raised. Is it a simply a phenomenon of intense, long-term activity, or is there a more direct connection to the actual business of running? A simple Google search of runner's high found over two million hits. A similar search for swimmer's high resulted in around 674,000 hits. A biker's high search resulted in 1.8 million hits, but many seemed to be focused on a world that is not self-propelled, but machine driven. A quick perusal of the initial hits seemed to suggest that any prolonged activity could result in a feeling of being high or euphoric. But, I began to wonder, why is it that after my years of activity in all three disciplines, it was only the runner's high that I had really experienced or heard much about?

Many potential reasons abound regarding this observation. One could simply be that it was I paid greater attention to something that I grown up hearing in a household and community where swimming and biking were largely overshadowed by the use of running as a fitness activity. Or maybe it had more to do with the fact that both biking and running largely depends on the artificiality of indoors (i.e., lap swimming) or the mechanics of cycling whereas running in its purest sense resulted in the athlete being a conduit of the world in which he or she traversed. Among many others, though, one thought continued to persist that made running truly unique in regards to all fitness disciplines. No matter the landscape, no matter the climate, no matter the resources, running was and remains an option for all. Where there is no water, where bikes are inconceivable in cost and utility, running remains available, even in the harshest of winters and the most blistering of summers, even in communities miles above the sea and those deep in the tropical jungles or where water is incredibly scarce and dangerous. Like the most basic, and beautiful gifts of our Maker, whether it be the gift of community or of love, running offers itself to all.

✝ ✝ ✝ ✝

Days and weeks after my experience on the golf course, I began to watch my children run more carefully. With great jubilance and off their heels, they gallivanted so quickly in this way, much like a dear friend of mine seems to do no matter where he is going. They were joyful, and I wasn't sure if they were running because of their joy or if their joy had much to do with running. Just a couple of days after my transcendent moment at the golf course, I found myself reflecting deeply on the experience. The message I had heard that day seemed very clear: *Running was intentionally granted by God and is associated with Christianity as a unique way to harmonize mind, body, and soul with the natural law and our divine nature, and in the process, provides opportunities for a deep sense of gratitude within an extended period of euphoria.*

Although I understood clearly what I heard that day, I recognized that most who heard me speak of this would quickly question the sanity of this assertion. But, I kept thinking that if the researchers were right, and we as humans were specifically designed for the purpose of running, AND we are made in the image and likeness of God, then wouldn't it mean that the ability to run was intentionally granted by our Maker. And if I was to take this a step further, and suggest that our runner capacity was not just for utilitarian reasons, but potentially for psychological, social, emotional, and/or transcendent/spiritual purposes, then suddenly the logic of it all suggests one crazy idea: God is telling us, in completely literal terms, that we should run towards Him, and that if we do, we will find Him in the process.

But before I got too caught up in my own twisted logic, I decided to go straight to one authority that preceded any thoughts I had by almost 2,000 years: the New Testament. And this is where the story got really, really interesting.

The approach was very simple. Plug the word run or ran (allowing for any variance) into the New American online version of the Gospels, then moving onto Acts of the Apostles, and eventually working through all of the books of the New Testament. If running really was part of the New Covenant, I was curious what I would find. Little did I know the chills that would arise as I set off on this endeavor.

The first interesting finding was that in the Gospels and the Acts of the Apostles, only **ran** (or a variant) was used. The word **run** (or variants) was nowhere to be found. Although presumably this would make sense to some extent, as these stories detail the past actions of Christ and his Apostles, it seemed somewhat curious that no counsel had been given by Christ or others to run at all, even in a metaphorical sense. But once these books had passed, and the subsequent Letters and Epistles of the New Testament took over, the opposite became true. **Ran** never appeared again, with one peculiar exception (Jude 1:11). "Woe unto them! For they went in the way of Cain, and **ran** riotously in the error of Balaam for hire, and perished in the gainsaying of Korah" (However, other translations replaced **ran** with "abandoned"). **Run** took over in all the passages. Again, arguments could easily be made that these particular books focused on giving advice for current and future people (thus **run** over **ran**) just as the first five books (Gospels/Acts) focused on telling stories of what had happened in the past. But even so, if we took the words **ran** and **run** literally, not figuratively, then it might seem rather prescriptive for our lives. And this is where things just became fascinating.

In all four Gospels, in eleven different passages, the word (or variant) of **ran** was always used in the context of faith, of fervor, of excitement, of joy, and of love. In Matthew 28:8, "And they departed quickly from the tomb with fear and great joy, and **ran** to bring his disciples word." John 20:4. "And they **ran** both together: and the other disciple out**ran** Peter, and came first to the tomb." Mark 5:6. "And when he saw Jesus from afar, he **ran** and worshipped him." Luke 19:4. "And he **ran** on before, and climbed up into a sycamore [sic] tree to see him: for he was to pass that way." Over and over, the passages spoke of running to Christ and running to spread the Word. Despite all of the threats the Apostles encountered during this time, never once was there a mention that they **ran** from others or because of fear. Even a review of the five passages (a sixth passage including ran was referring to a ship hitting shore) that included **ran** (or variant) in the Acts of the Apostles, no clear mention of running due to fear was noted. Although passages mentioned people's running towards Paul in anger (e.g., 21:30, "And all the city was moved, and the people **ran** together; and they laid hold on Paul, and dragged him out of the temple: and straightway the doors were shut"), even in two similar passages such as these, running was used as a means of being closer to Christ's apostles albeit in an aggressive manner. In the rest of the passages, running was once again depicted as a means of being closer the Word of God. Although other words (e.g., fled) could have been used to denote a rapid escape, the most basic connotation of the word **ran** remained positive.

Just as the Gospel & Acts seemed to convey a sense of how running was used in search of love and the truth, and not fear and despair, so the advice put forth in the subsequent Epistles and Letters seemed to echo a pathway of meaning and joy, not sorrow, isolation, or fear. Except for the previously mentioned verse in Jude (using **ran**, not **run**), the eight passages spoken in these books suggest a virtuous means through running. Two of the most beautiful appear in Corinthians 1, (9:24) "Know ye not that they that **run** in a race run all, but one receiveth the prize? Even so **run**; that ye may attain"; (9:26) "I therefore so **run**, as not uncertainly; so fight I, as not beating the air." In Philippians 2:16, it states "...holding fast the word of life, so that in the day of Christ I will have reason to glory because I did not **run** in vain nor toil in vain." Hebrews 12:1 says, "Therefore let us also, seeing we are compassed about with so great a cloud of witnesses, lay aside every weight, and the sin which doth so easily beset us, and let us **run** with patience the race that is set before us." And in maybe the most striking passage of all, Thessalonians 3:1 proclaims, "Finally, brethren, pray for us, that the word of the Lord may **run** and be glorified, even as also it is with you."

In my short life, I had always heard passages such as these couched in many analogous terms, and expressed in ways that suggested that we should always go quickly and fervently towards whatever Christ calls us to do. That we should have a sense of urgency about our purpose on earth, and not languish in the uncertainty which this world brings, but always move forward with His call. But never before that one quiet, cold, solitary early morning in January had I ever thought once that maybe, just maybe, we were called to take those words just as they were said.

With that, my journey of exploration continues, with one side note. I wondered that if I was correct, and running was directly associated with the New Covenant, then did that mean that a change had occurred from the Old Covenant, when running was equated with fear, not love. So I set out to explore the books of Old Testament, but quickly became derailed when I struggled to find online versions for many that allowed for an easy search of the operative words **run** or **ran** (or variants). But before this pursuit ended for now, I did come across the first line in which **run** or **ran** had been used in the book of Genesis opening the Old Testament. In Chapter 16, Verse 6 of the New American Version online, it says:

"Abram told Sarai: 'Your maid is in your power. Do to her whatever you please.' Sarai then abused her so much that Hagar **ran** away from her."

It sure keeps me wondering anyway...

† † † †

When I set out to write this book, I didn't know I was writing a book. Over the course of a few years, thoughts and ideas would become articles and reflections until I realized one day that they all possessed a similar thread. The thread was life in its rawest form, and my attempt to understand just what made life so meaningful for many, and so meaningless for others. It is a journey that I will continue until I die, and then hopefully by the grace of God, my questions will be answered and my love will be complete. In the meantime, what I repeatedly have found is that the older I get, the more questions I have and the less answers I possess. But what I have come to know full well, not from myself, but from the collective wisdom of the ages through His wisdom, is that the meaning of life is somewhere deep, deep within the throngs of life itself, lived moment by moment, sorrow by sorrow, joy by joy.

I surmised that if I was to be privileged with a glimpse of what life really had to offer, I must set out to do things in raw form. I must expose myself daily to the elements, such as running or biking to work or hiking the trails. I must ride the bus, and listen intently to people, in and out of my office, who could impart me with wisdom that my life did not possess. I must use technology as an asset, but not immersively, and find pockets of time daily where no words or wavelength could reach me. In the same way, I reckoned that if what I was going to compose was truly authentic to the human experience, then I must do it in all places. On six degree, snowy runs. One hundred and eight degree, rainy bikes. In front of crying parents. With kids draped over my shoulder reading what I was typing, and wrestling and screaming around me. I was tempted to pull away at times from my daily life to a secure place to write, but something (actually, I hope, Someone) spoke to me and said that if what I was writing was authentic and worthwhile, it would stand the test of climate and chaos and a cacophony of screams. I hope it did.

We are living in an interesting time, one in which many experts predict that the division between virtual and reality will continue to blur. I find this strangely ironic. What gaming manufacturers, and social networking sites, and television stations are seeking to do is to give us the utmost, lifelike experience of the most dramatic, amazing kind. Much of this promise is that it comes with no strings attached. This of course is not true, but that is a subject for another time. But the great irony is that what the virtual world is really trying to give us is another life, just like the one available to us now. For those who want to love authentically, it is available, but always at a price. For those who want to be soldier, it is available, but of course with some or the ultimate cost. For those who want to climb a mountain, that is possible, but of course with definite risk. All real life comes with risks and costs. Just ask Him. Anything that comes with the promise of none is not a life at all.

As we risk pulling ourselves out of our own lives, and rendering those four dimensions of our being into a semi-permeable shell—a stranger staring back in the mirror, there still remains a promise that beckons (2 Peter 1: 2-3):

> Grace and peace be multiplied to you in the knowledge of God and of Jesus our Lord; seeing that His divine power has granted to us everything pertaining to life and

godliness, through the true knowledge of Him who called us by His own glory and excellence.

If we can come to believe this, then it appears that life is there for the taking in whatever pathway we are called. Pray that you and I shed our fear and our pride, embrace change that must come, joys and sorrows that will arise, in our long run to the One that is all.

Amen.

Notes

Chapter 2: The Fear of Fear

1. Cartwright-Hatton, S., McNicol, K., & Doubleday, E. (2006). Anxiety in a neglected population: Prevalence of anxiety disorders in pre-adolescent children. *Clinical Psychology Review, 26,* 817–833. doi: 10.1016/j.cpr.2005.12.002

2. Muris, P., & Steerneman, P. (2001). The Revised version of the Screen for Child Anxiety Related Emotional Disorders (SCARED-R): First evidence for its reliability and validity in a clinical sample. *British Journal of Clinical Psychology, 40,* 35-44.

Chapter 3: The Root of All Vices

1. Brummelman, E., Thomaes, S., Overbeek, G., Orobio de Castro, B., Van den Hout, M.A., & Bushman, B.J. (2014) On feeding those hungry for praise: Person praise backfires in children with low self-esteem. *Journal of Experimental Psychology: General, 143,* 9-14. http://dx.doi.org/10.1037/a0031917

Chapter 4: In Letting Out the Spirit Within

1. Tonioni, F., D'Alessandris, L., Lai C, Martinelli, D., Corvino, S., Vasale, M., Fanella, F., Aceto, P., & Bria P. (2012) Internet addiction: hours spent online, behaviors and psychological symptoms. *General Hospital Psychiatry, 34,* 80-87. There are numerous

articles and chapters looking at the connection between behavioral and substance addictions, but here is one.

Chapter 5: Resolving to Make This Year Mean More

1. Musick, M., & and Wilson, J. (2003) Volunteering and Depression: The Role of Psychological and Social Resources in Different Age Groups. *Social Science and Medicine 56,* 259-269;

2. Thoits, P., & and Hewitt, L. (2001) Volunteer Work and Social Well-being. *Journal of Health and Social Behavior 48,* 174-187.

3. Clark, S. (2003) Voluntary Work Benefits Mental Health. *A Life in The Day 7,* 10-14. Further articles are available regarding the link between volunteering and mental health and well-being.

4. W. Kip Viscusi, *Smoking: Making the Risky Decision* (New York: Oxford University Press, 1992), pp. 61-78.

Chapter 6: Dear Family & Friends: My Apologies...

1. Sanbonmatsu, D.M., Strayer, D.L., Medeiros-Ward, N., & Watson, J.M. (2013) Who multi-tasks and why? Multi-Tasking ability, perceived multi-tasking ability, impulsivity, and sensation seeking. *PLoS ONE 8*: e54402. doi:10.1371/journal.pone.0054402

2. "New Mobile Obsession U.S. Teens Triple Data Usage":
   Nielsen. December 15, 2011.
   http://www.nielsen.com/us/en/insights/news/2011/n
   ew-mobile-obsession-u-s-teens-triple-data-usage.html

3. Twenge, J.M., Gentile, B., DeWall, C.N., Ma, D.,
   Lacefield, K., & Schurtz, D.R. (2010). Birth cohort
   increases in psychopathology among young Americans,
   1938-2007: A cross-temporal meta-analysis of the
   MMPI. *Clinical Psychology Review, 30*, 145-152.

4. Land, K.C, Lamb, V.L., & Zheng, H. (2011). How are the
   kids doing? How do we know? Recent trends in child
   and youth well-being in the United States and some
   international comparisons. *Social Indicators Research
   100,* 463-477.

5. Romer, D., Jamieson, P.E., Bushman, B.J., Bleakley, A.,
   Wang, A., Langleben, D., & Jamieson, K.H. (2014)
   Parental Desensitization to Violence and Sex in Movies.
   Pediatrics, 134, 877-884.

Chapter 7: The Day the Silence Died

1. "After PS4 and Xbox One releases Sony and Microsoft
   must learn nothing endures but change." *The
   National: Business.* December 23, 2013.
   http://www.thenational.ae/business/industry-
   insights/media/after-ps4-and-xbox-one-releases-sony-
   and-microsoft-must-learn-nothing-endures-but-change

Chapter 8: The Three Pillars of Health

1. Bennett-Johnson, S. (2011). Addressing the obesity epidemic: Don't blame the victim. *Psychology Monitor, 43,* 5.

2. "Train Your Body to Fuel Efficiently." Triathlete. January 7, 2015. http://triathlon.competitor.com/2015/01/training/avoid-the-wall-with-fasting-runs_92125

Chapter 9: In Search of a Hundred Miles of Gratitude

1. McDougall, Christopher (2009). *Born to Run.* New York: Random House. On page 239, the author describes a study done by Dr. Dennis Bramble at the University of Utah.

Chapter 10: We Are What We Eat

1. Robinson T.N., Borzekowski D.G., Matheson D.M., & Kraemer H.C. (2007) Effects of Fast Food Branding on Young Children's Taste Preferences. *Archives of Pediatric & Adolescent Medicine, 161*: 792-797. http://abcnews.go.com/Health/Healthday/story?id=4508191

2. Enns C.W., Mickle S.J., & Goldman J.D. (2003) Trends in food and nutrient intakes by adolescents in the United States. *Family Economic Nutrition Review,* 15, 15–27.

3. Understanding Childhood Obesity. 2011 Statistical Sourcebook. American Heart Association / American Stroke Association.

4. Pollan, Michael (2006). *The Omnivore's Dilemma: A Natural History of Four Meals.* New York: Penguin.

5. Jacka F.N., Ystrom E., Brantsaeter A.L., Karevold E., Roth C., Haugen M., Meltzer H.M., & Berk M. (2013) Maternal and early postnatal nutrition and mental health of offspring by age 5 years: A prospective cohort study *Journal of the American Academy of Child and Adolescent Psychiatry, 52,* 1038-1047. http://www.medscape.com/viewarticle/809767 (Stop the Pop: Soda Linked to Aggression, Inattention in Kids).

Chapter 11: There's More to Sleep Than Shuts the Eye

1. Chase, R. M., & Pincus, D. B. (2011). Sleep-related problems in children and adolescents with anxiety disorders. *Behavioral Sleep Medicine, 9,* 224-236. doi: 10.1080/15402002.2011606768

2. Paavonen, E.J., Raikkonen, K., Lahti J., Komsi, N., Heinonen, K., Pesonen, A.K., Jarvenpaa, A.L., Strandberg, T., Kajantie, E., & Porkka-Heiskanen, T.(2009). Short sleep duration and behavioral symptoms of attention-deficit/hyperactivity disorder in healthy 7- to 8-year-old children, *Pediatrics, 123*: e857–e864.

3. Stix, G. "Sleeps Role in Obesity, Schizophrenia, Diabetes...Everything." December 20, 2013. *Scientific American.* http://blogs.scientificamerican.com/talking-

back/2013/12/20/sleeps-role-in-obesity-schizophrenia-diabetes-everything/

4. Bell, J.F., & Zimmerman, F. J (2010). Shortened nighttime sleep duration in early life and subsequent childhood obesity. *Archives of Pediatric & Adolescent Medicine, 164,* 840-845.

5. Petrovsky, N., Ettinger, U., Hill, A., Frenzel, L., Meyhöfer, I., Wagner, M., Backhaus, J., & Kumari, V. (2014). Sleep Deprivation Disrupts Prepulse Inhibition and Induces Psychosis-Like Symptoms in Healthy Humans. *The Journal of Neuroscience, 34*: 9134-9140; doi: 10.1523

6. Fosse, M.J., Fosse, R., Hobson, J.A., Stickgold, R.J. (2003). Dreaming and episodic memory: a functional dissociation? *Journal of Cognitive Neuroscience, 15*:1-9.

7. Scheen, A.J., Byrne, M.M., Plat, L., Leproult, R., & Van Cauter, E. (1996). Relationships between sleep quality and glucose regulation in normal humans. *American Journal of Physiology, 15*:1-9

8. Chong, Y., Fryar, C.D., & Gu, Q, (2013) Prescription Sleep Aid Use Among Adults: United States, 2005–2010. NCS Data Brief

9. Russo, A., Miller, K., Marder, W. (2008) Prescription sleep aid use in young adults. *Thomson Reuters Research Brief.*

10. Lauderdale, D.S., Knutson, K.L., Yan, L.L., Rathouz, P.J., Hulley, S.B., Sidney, S., & Liu, K. (2006). Objectively

measured sleep characteristics among early-middle-aged adults: The CARDIA study. *American Journal of Epidemiology, 164,* 5–16.

11. Mindell, J. A. & Owens, J. A. (2010). *A Clinical Guide to Pediatric Sleep: Diagnosis and Management of Sleep Problems.* (2nd ed.) Philadelphia, PA: Lippincott, Willians, & Wilkins.

Chapter 12: Partner Bill of Rights

1. World Bank. 1993. Investing in health: World development indicators: World Development Report. New York: Oxford University Press.

2. World Health Organization. 1997. Violence against women: A priority health issue. Accessed April, 8 2008.

3. Full Report of the Prevalence, Incidence, and Consequences of Violence Against Women, Department of Justice, 2000.

4. Peek-Asa, C., Wallis, A., Harland, K., Beyer, K., Dickey P, & Saftlas A. (2011). Rural disparity in domestic violence prevalence and access to resources. *Journal of Women's Health, 20,* 1743-1749.

5. Extent, Nature, and Consequences of Intimate Partner Violence, Department of Justice, 2000.

Chapter 13: The Almighty Word

1. Wynne, L.C. & Singer, M.T. (1963). Thought disorder and family relations of schizophrenics. I. A research strategy. *Archives of General Psychiatry, 9,* 191-198.

2. Roisko, R., Wahlberg, K.E., Miettunen, J., & Tienari, P. (2014). Association of parental communication deviance with offspring's psychiatric and thought disorders. A systematic review and meta-analysis. *European Psychiatry, 29,* 20-31.

Chapter 14: Striving for the Ideal—In Others

1. Walsh, R. (2011). Lifestyle and Mental Health. *American Psychologist, 66*, 579-592.

2. http://www.freerepublic.com/focus/f-news/1091777/posts. "A Good Wife's Guide." *Housekeeping Monthly.* Published May 13, 1955.

Chapter 15: Where Mental Health Begins

1. http://www.medscape.com/viewarticle/820011. Top 100 Selling Drugs of 2013. Medscape Medical News. Megan Brooks. Published January 30, 2014.

2. Hamp, A., Stamm, K, Christidis, P., & Nigrinis, A. (2014). Are psychologists in the states that have the most mental illness?, *Monitor in Psychology, 45,* 13.

Chapter 16: Turning Distress into Joy

1. http://www.virtuesforlife.com/father-forgives-sons-killer/ (see video imbedded in article entitled "Father Forgives Son's Killer" published on *Virtues for Life* website)

2. Worthington, E. L., Jr., Witvliet, C. V. O., Pietrini, P., & Miller, A. J. (2007). Forgiveness, health, and well-being: A review of evidence for emotional versus decisional forgiveness, dispositional forgivingness, and reduced unforgiveness. *Journal of Behavioral Medicine, 30,* 291–302.

3. Lundahl, B.W., Taylor, M.J., Stevenson, R., & Roberts K.D. (2008) Process-based forgiveness interventions: A meta-analytic review. *Research on Social Work Practice, 18,* 465–478.

4. Field, C., Zander, J., & Hall, G. (2013). 'Forgiveness is a present to yourself as well': An intrapersonal model of forgiveness in victims of violent crime. *International Review of Victimology, 19,* 235-247.

5. Mukashema, I., & Mullet, E. (2013). Unconditional forgiveness, reconciliation sentiment, and mental health among victims of genocide in Rwanda. *Social Indicators Research, 113,* 121–132.

6. http://www.foxnews.com/us/2010/12/31/addict-turned-ironman-swims-bikes-runs-past/ "Addict-Turned-Ironman Swims, Bikes, Runs from Past". Published December 31, 2010. *Associated Press*

7. Smith, T. W. (1992). Hostility and Health: Current Status of a Psychosomatic Hypothesis. *Health Psychology*, *11*, 139–150.

8. Frost, B., Ko, Chia-Huei, E., & James, L.R. (2007) Implicit and explicit personality: A test of a channeling hypothesis for aggressive behavior. *Journal of Applied Psychology, 92,* 1299–1319.

9. www.stmarys.org/articles-1. November 2012 edition of *Just Thinking*. "Having It All Without Having It All." Jim Schroeder

10. Rosenberg, M., & McCullough, B.C. (1981). Mattering: Inferred significance and mental health. *Research in Community and Mental Health, 2*, 163 – 182.

11. Piliavin, J.A., & Siegl, E. (2007). Health benefits of volunteering in the Wisconsin longitudinal study. *Journal of Health and Social Behavior, 48*, 450-464.

12. http://www.people.com/people/archive/article/0,,20287120,00.html. A Serial Killer's Sole Survivor. *People Magazine*. Published June 29, 2009

13. http://overcomingsexualabuse.com/2010/08/08/the-dangers-of-gratitude-and-a-positive-attitude/. The Dangers of Gratitude and a Positive Attitude. *Overcoming Sexual Abuse: Embracing a New Life.* August 8, 2010.

14. Park, N., Peterson, C., & Seligman, M.E.P. (2005). *Character strengths in forty nations and fifty states.* Unpublished manuscript, University of Rhode Island.

15. Emmons, R. A. (2013). *Gratitude works! A twenty-one day program for creating emotional prosperity.* San Francisco: Jossey-Bass.

16. Emmons, R. A. (2007). *Thanks! How the new science of gratitude can make you happier.* New York: Houghton-Mifflin.

17. Seligman, M.E.P., Steen, T.A., Park, N., & Peterson, C. (2005). Positive psychology progress: Empirical validation of interventions. *American Psychologist, 60,* 410–421.

18. Kashdan, T.B., Uswatte, G., & Julian, T. (2006). Gratitude and hedonic and eudaimonic wellbeing in Vietnam war veterans. *Behaviour Research and Therapy, 44,* 177-199.

19. Vernon, L.L., Dillon, J.M., & Steiner, A.R.W. (2009). Proactive coping, gratitude, and posttraumatic stress disorder in college women. *Anxiety, Stress, and Coping, 22,* 117-127.

20. Emmons, R.A., & Stern, R. (2013). Gratitude as a psychotherapeutic intervention. *Journal of Clinical Psychology: In Session, 69,* 846–855.

21. http://www.kipp.org/ (Knowledge is Power Program)

22. Skogrand, L., Singh, A., Allgood, S., DeFrain, J., Defrain, N., & Jones, J.E. (2007). The process of transcending a traumatic childhood. *Contemporary Family Therapy, 29,* 253-270.

23. Grossman, F.K., Sorsoli, L., & Kia-Keating, M. (2006). A gale force wind: Meaning making by male survivors of childhood sexual abuse. *American Journal of Orthopsychiatry, 76,* 434-443.

24. Staub, E., & Vollhardt, J. (2008). Altruism born of suffering: The roots of caring and helping after victimization and other trauma. *American Journal of Orthopsychiatry, 78,* 267-280.

25. Grossman, F.K., Sorsoli, L., & Kia-Keating, M. (2006). A gale force wind: Meaning making by male survivors of childhood sexual abuse. *American Journal of Orthopsychiatry, 76,* 434-443.

26. Heintzelman, S.J. & King, L.A. (2014). Life is pretty meaningful. *American Psychologist, 69,* 561-574.

27. Keyes, C.L.M. (2002). The mental health continuum: From languishing to flourishing in life. *Journal of Health and Social Research, 43,* 207-222.

Chapter 18: Why Oh Why?

1. Wortman, C.B., & Silver, R. (1989). The myths of coping with loss. *Journal of Consulting and Clinical Psychology, 57,* 349-357.

Chapter 19: Just What Happiness Are We Seeking?

1. Seligman, M.E.P (2002). *Authentic Happiness.* New York: Free Press.

2. Peterson, C., Park, N., & Seligman, M.E.P (2005a). Assessment of character strengths. In G.P. Koocher, J.C. Norcross, & S.S. Hill III (Eds.), *Psychologists' desk reference* (2nd ed., pp. 93-98). New York: Oxford University Press.

3. Peterson, C., & Seligman, M.E.P (2004). *Character strengths and virtues: A handbook and classification.* Washington, DC: American Psychological Association.

Epilogue: Running to Him

1. Bramble, D., & Lieberman, D. (2004). Endurance running and the evolution of homo. *Nature, 432,*345-352.

2. http://www.runnersworld.com/trail-runner-profiles/trail-yiannis-kouros?page=single. "On the Trail with Yiannis Kouros." *Running Times.* Published April 4, 2006. Adam Chase.

3. http://www.nytimes.com/2008/03/27/health/nutrition/27best.html?_r=2&. "Yes, Running Can Make You High." *New York Times.* Published March 27, 2008. Gina Kolata.

Made in the USA
Lexington, KY
05 June 2019